CW00794747

PHOTOGRAPHY AT SEA

**ADLARD
COLES
NAUTICAL**

PATRICK ROACH & FRED BARTER

PHOTOGRAPHY AT SEA

TECHNIQUES FOR CAPTURING AMAZING PHOTOGRAPHS AFLOAT

Contents

Published by Adlard Coles Nautical
an imprint of A & C Black Publishers Ltd
36 Soho Square, London WID 3QY
www.adlardcoles.com

Copyright © Patrick Roach & Fred Barter 2009

First edition published 2009

ISBN: 978-1-4081-1202-1

All rights reserved. No part of this publication may be reproduced in any form or by
any means – graphic, electronic or mechanical, including photocopying, recording, taping
or information storage and retrieval systems – without the prior permission in writing
of the publishers.

The right of the author to be identified as the author of this work has been asserted by
him in accordance with the Copyright, Designs and Patents Act, 1988.

A CIP catalogue record for this book is available from the British Library.

This book is produced using paper that is made from wood grown in managed,
sustainable forests. It is natural, renewable and recyclable. The logging and
manufacturing processes conform to the environmental regulations of the
country of origin.

Design and concept by Fred Barter at Bosun Press

Typeset in 11pt Gill Sans light
Printed and bound in China by C&C Offset Printing Co

The most important tools a photographer has are his eyes, the ability to see a potential picture, see and review the details, and move around to find a better position, to remove all distracting elements and to have patience to wait for the very best light. All of these are only seen through the creative photographer's eyes....

Patrick Roach

Foreword

Patrick Roach is one of my favourite photographers. He is a supreme professional and has specialised in taking pictures at sea for over 30 years. He started work as an assistant to Terence Donovan in the Sixties. Donovan was one of the two photographers of that time who turned the world of fashion photography on its head; the other was David Bailey. Between them they ousted the previous generation with a series of outrageous pictures that broke all the rules. *Vogue* magazine was the first to use them and both became celebrities known to a much wider world than the industry in which they worked.

Donovan, as well as being extremly creative, was a hard taskmaster. Patrick Roach's job was to get the technical stuff right, lighting in place, exposures double checked, props placed, everything ready for the boss to use his eye to create the picture. That is what photography is really about – the eye of the photographer. His tools are the camera and light. Photography has even been called painting with light.

Patrick Roach learnt his trade with one of the best but does his own thing now, specialising in the sea and the boats he loves. Throughout this book we want to show how and why Patrick selects his subjects.

You will find location and technical information about each picture on pages 157–160.

You may simply wish to take better pictures for yourself, family and friends, in which case the advice that Patrick gives here will enhance your work. In any case, we hope you enjoy looking at these superb pictures. Take Patrick's advice: always have a camera with you. If there is no camera, there are no photographs.

Fred Barter

Introduction

This is a book about taking photographs at sea. To get the most from your time afloat your camera should be considered as a permanent fixture, almost as important as your echo sounder and charts. Anyone who is lucky enough to experience the thrill that comes from being on the water has a chance to share their good fortune with others later. A photograph has the power to stimulate more than our visual senses. With a dash of imagination it is possible to hear the roar of surf, smell the air and feel the sun. All you need to do is follow a few basic photographic rules.

Unlike professionals who are expected to get first-class results every time they press the shutter, an amateur photographer has the advantage of time. Remember you are free to take as long as you like. Without the pressures of budgets and client briefs you too could produce pictures of this standard.

The main requirement is a basic understanding of how your equipment operates. Read the instruction book. It may not be the most exciting narrative in the world but it's important. Only when you have experimented with the camera controls and understood the true function of each feature will you be ready to get the most out of this book.

Explore the capabilities of the new generation of digital cameras. They have removed the need for much technical knowledge, finding the correct exposure, getting the shot in focus; all this is done for you. The only other skill you need is your eye and your imagination.

Patrick Roach

Digital photography

Photography today has been revolutionised. The digital camera now allows us to achieve results that are technically superb. Unfortunately the important factor that the camera cannot provide is the photographer's eye. This book looks at the important subject of composition and the reasons why one picture is better than another. We look at the automatic functions that your digital camera offers. We then progress to the more technical options whereby you can control exposure, focus, speed etc to achieve even better photographs.

Digital cameras are available from the small and relatively inexpensive to highly sophisticated professional cameras with special lenses, filters and extra memory. The small compact digital camera is capable of producing many of the photographs in this book. But, as is often the case, if you pay a little more you can get even better results. For the serious amateur photographer this may be tempting. We explain how to take good pictures with simple step-by-step instructions. Luckily digital cameras share common features so, although we have used a single camera to demonstrate the various controls, they should be easy to identify on whatever camera you own. 'Keep it simple' is a motto that I firmly believe in, and if sailing with friends

Digital cameras tend to use the same controls as each other. In this book we have used the Panasonic Lumix to explain the functions.

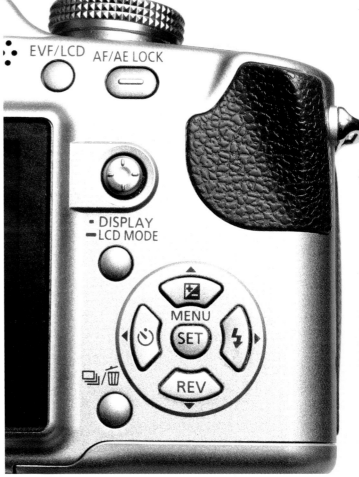

I happily tuck my digital inside my oilskins, snapping away merrily when it's least expected. Bearing this in mind, I rarely recommend spending large sums of hard-earned money; quite the opposite.

Armed with your choice of camera you now need to consider your main objective. Over an average season you will experience a variety of different situations on the water: sailing with friends, skippering your own boat, exploring abroad, an annual cruise or just a day's sail pottering around anchorages. Imagine what each might have to offer and try to pick out the photographically interesting sections. Step-by-step the images will build

into a master album. Your ultimate aim should be to produce the perfect reminder of a day or a week well spent.

The instruction manual

This is a double-edged sword, often mind-bogglingly dull but absolutely essential to understanding the camera functions. There will be features that won't be fully-appreciated the first time round but, having read and understood them, will come into their own at a later stage. In this book we will try to simplify the process.

The mode dial

Preparing to take a picture

There are several adjustments you can make to ensure that the best possible result is achieved. These are found in the mode settings which can be seen on the monitor window at the back of your camera. It is worth taking time to understand the options. Or you can set the camera to automatic and it will record the scene before you.

My camera is almost always set on aperture priority. This gives me control of the depth of focus. I usually need to have pinpoint sharpness just on the subject. It's worth remembering to keep an eye on the speed reading, if there is one, in your viewfinder.

Sometimes luck plays a part and here the sun picks out the yacht sailing in blustery conditions. With a bit too much canvas it's hairy for the crew, but for me it's a terrific shot, showing the power sail can generate.

The mode dial on top of the camera.

The monitor screen on the back of the camera.

As the mode dial is turned the various controls are highlighted.

The mode dial takes you to the many functions that a digital camera offers.

Basic: the simplest way to take pictures

iA Intelligent auto mode. This allows the camera to handle all settings for taking pictures.

P The exposure is automatically adjusted by the camera.

Advanced

A Aperture priority. The shutter speed is automatically determined by the aperture value you set.

S Shutter priority. The aperture value is automatically determined by the shutter speed you set.

M Manual exposure mode. The exposure is adjusted by the aperture value and shutter speed, which are manually set.

Custom Custom mode used to take pictures with previously-registered settings.

Movies Motion picture mode. Allows you to record motion pictures.

Print Print mode. Use this to print pictures.

SCN Scene mode. Allows you to take pictures that match the scene being recorded.

Setting the camera menu

After a long sail in hot conditions it's tempting to break out your favourite tipple. But instead, get into the dinghy for a few minutes and potter around the anchorage. Get some different views, especially of your own yacht, perhaps in a unique setting.

This shot could easily be taken in sunset mode if you have it. I used aperture priority and took the meter reading by pointing the central part of the viewfinder away from the centre of the sun – the orange area – in order not to make it a complete silhouette. You need to experiment with the exposure but one of the luxuries of all digital cameras is that you can view the results immediately.

I framed the yacht off-centre to take in the land and centre the quickly-setting sun. This gave a reflection all the way from horizon to camera, the silhouetted yacht adding to the impact.

Setting the menu for taking control over the camera functions

There are various menu screens that will appear on your LCD monitor. Consult your instruction manual for information specific to your camera.

These may include:

- White balance
- White balance adjustment
- Intelligent ISO
- Sensitivity
- Aspect ratio

These menu screens enable you to take control when the pictures you wish to take have specific factors which the basic intelligent auto function can't handle. We go through these options and their benefits in more detail on other pages.

In this book we cannot take you through these features in detail for all cameras but, by reading your instruction manual, you should be able to understand how to override the automatic functions available.

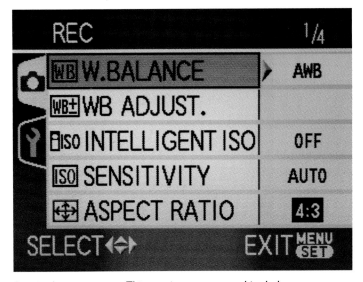

A typical menu screen. This one is set to auto white balance.

This shot was taken with a 300mm lens set to its widest aperture – f4, to get the fastest possible shutter speed to freeze the fast moving motor boat.

To get the best possible colour information into your picture, your camera's sensor has to work out the colour temperature of the current light. This is under the menu option called white balance. Most of the time it's easiest to leave this setting on auto but if it's a sunny day try setting it to daylight, as this usually gives a slightly better colour rendition. If you are photographing in cloudy conditions your image will definitely benefit by using the cloud setting on the white balance menu.

Look at the various lighting options for your camera and try to remember them. Don't forget to alter the settings when the lighting conditions change, or the next time you use the camera.

The LCD monitor and viewfinder

There are two ways to frame or compose pictures: through the screen monitor or through the eye piece, also known as the viewfinder. Many camera manufacturers do not include a viewfinder but just expect the owner to use the rear screen monitor to compose the shot. I guess that this has something to do with cost, but I consider this a major flaw.

I find it impossible in daylight to see the image accurately let alone make a sensible composition. Some viewfinders also have read-outs in them which are a further help and save you checking the shutter speed on the monitor. With no light shining on them, monitors alone are usable but you lose the intimacy that a viewfinder gives and this is needed to create your picture.

This typical setting in these rugged harbours along the Brittany coast seems to convey the peace that often comes from pottering around boats. There is a myriad of odd angles and a sense that the boats are just sleeping, waiting for the incoming tide to bob around their moorings once more.

The purpose of the grid is to ensure the picture is horizontal.

Composing the picture

There are two ways to compose the picture in the frame. The LCD monitor offers a large screen and the viewfinder is an eyepiece which you look through. Both have their advantages and disadvantages. The LCD monitor will give a big picture but is subject to the available ambient light. In some circumstances it will be too bright to see the monitor's image. The viewfinder blocks out any ambient light and makes it much easier to concentrate on composing the picture. Most experienced photographers would prefer to use the viewfinder.

In recording mode

Information can be displayed on the LCD monitor and through the viewfinder, which tells you about the camera's settings and values relative to the picture you are about to take.

These can include:

- The current battery charge
- The histogram (which shows you whether your camera settings are likely to produce an acceptable picture)
- The exposure setting, lens aperture and shutter speed
- The ISO value
- The date and time

Once you understand the meaning of these terms the information display will help you take better pictures.

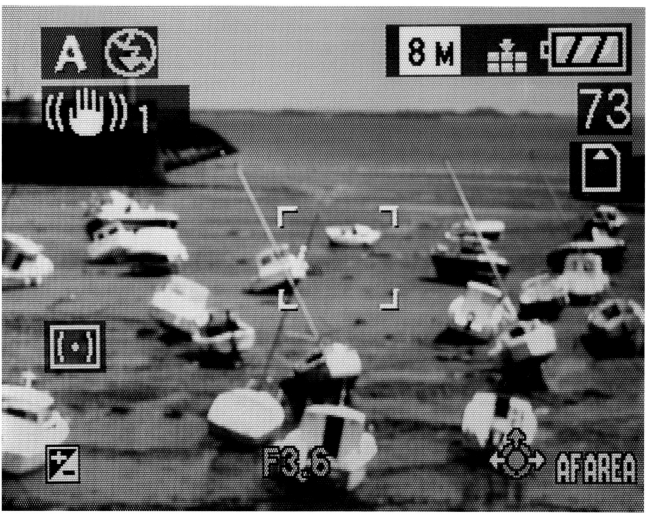

This screen shows you all the current settings on your camera. There is usually an option to clear this information off the screen so that you just see the picture.

The LCD monitor.

The viewfinder.

Taking pictures in automatic mode

Taking pictures in auto mode is the most popular way people use their cameras and that includes me! As long as I have a read-out of the exact exposure it allows me to concentrate on the action. Following a group of racing yachts into a mark is always going to provide some excitement, if only for the RIB driver as I tell him to get ever closer.

The three yachts in the foreground had a close battle and emerged in this tight formation. After they set their spinnakers I positioned myself ahead as they tore off on a reach with perfectly-set kites. The angles cause your eye to skim back across the page to the mark.

A stroll around a foreign harbour can throw up some unexpected images. Here the colourful fishing floats are just hanging off the stern of the boat, tightly framed with a hint of the marina in the background, or bottom right, fishing nets in a fine mesh. Try to include signs, boat names, notice boards etc, if only as a memory aid to the forgetful photographer.

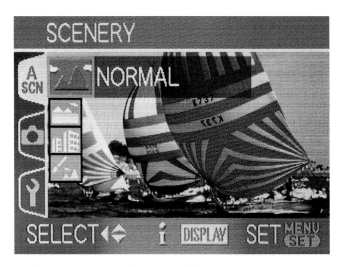
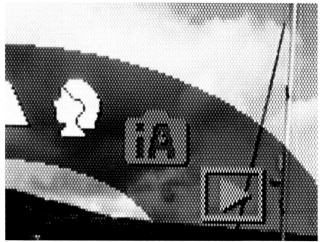

Intelligent auto mode will sort out all the settings you see on this picture above.

Taking pictures using intelligent auto mode

The beauty of a digital compact camera is that you can easily take it with you and capture the scenes that make a valuable addition to your sailing adventures.

The camera will set appropriate settings to match the scene. If you want to take pictures without altering the camera settings this is the mode to use.

The following functions are controlled in iA mode:

- Stabiliser – camera shake is detected and stabilised
- ISO sensitivity – the camera will control the shutter speed to match the movement of the subject and the surrounding brightness
- Face detection – the camera will automatically detect a person's face and will adjust focus and exposure to ensure a good picture
- Scene detection – options might include portraits, scenery, close-ups, night portraits and night scenery
- Continuous auto focus – the camera makes the picture sharp

You can also make some changes to settings in the intelligent auto mode such as aspect ratio, the proportions of the picture, the picture size, the degree of stabilisation, and colour effects.

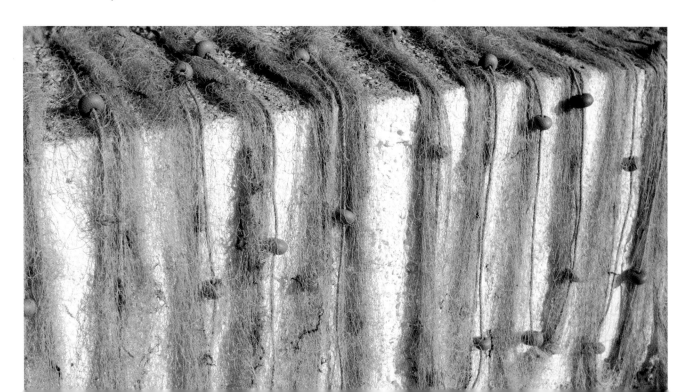

Plan your photography

Even if you don't always have the luxury of time, do try to spend a few moments thinking through what you want to achieve with your pictures. A bit of thought about conditions and preferred angles can help to make your photographs much better.

If the seas are bumpy as in this shot, positioning will be more difficult and the camera will need some protection. It was very difficult keeping the yacht in the frame, especially with the cropping.

I positioned myself ahead of the yacht, making sure my equipment was dry after the bouncy ride. I could see from the extreme angle of heel of this fast racing boat that there was going to be a brilliant angle from the leeward quarter, looking into the cockpit and along the deck. To enhance the impact of the picture, I chose a long lens and cropped in very tight. I have to admit that due to the rough conditions I shot several frames and only got the whole boat in this one.

Try to look at what you are photographing and ask if there is a better way, a different angle etc. My brief here was to produce an upright picture of a lighthouse for a magazine article. It would have been simple to take the obvious shot, but by standing close, angling the camera to look up and shooting with a wide angle lens, this striking image started to create something different.

When taking upright pictures it is best to hold the camera in this way, with the shutter at the bottom, always remembering to hold the camera firmly.

Taking pictures

The most important element of a good photograph is the composition. To be able to create good pictures you need to to be able to see opportunities. If you restrict yourself to pointing the camera at the family or your boat, the results will always be dull. You need to look for the moment when your subjects are relaxed, not frozen in awkward poses. Take the picture when the people are unaware and doing something else. Look at your boat from a new angle. Get down low. Check the background. Is it cluttered? Is your boat well lit? Is the sun behind and therefore in shadow, which means that some detail will be lost, or is the sun angle illuminating the boat, exposing all the detail? Consider the lighting conditions. Bright sunlight will give good detail but not always an emotive image.

Early mornings and late evenings can often provide a stunning photograph. Your intelligent auto mode will compensate for the lighting conditions. The best way to

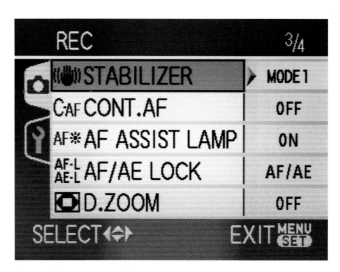

You will find a setting which helps reduce camera shake.

hold your camera is to lean against something solid and stand firmly with your feet slightly apart. Press the shutter halfway down to allow the camera to focus on your subject; be careful not to move the camera when you press the shutter button.

Common mistakes

Poor composition ruins many an interesting shot. Lack of concentration just before pressing the shutter can result in missed opportunities or, even worse, looking at your pictures afterwards you realise you have chopped off your mother's head.

Take time when framing the shot. Aim the AF area on the monitor screen at the point on which you want to focus.

When pressing the shutter, keep the pressure just firm enough to operate it, rather than using too much, or camera shake will spoil the picture.

Check your subjects are ready when photographing people, and don't keep on asking them to smile; it stops them being relaxed. They might even move out of the frame when close cropped so be aware if they are moving around or in action. Be patient; only take the shot if it looks good.

Try zooming in and out before taking the shot to see if you can improve it. Move around your subject; change the angle from flat-on to a more oblique view. This will give your picture depth, make features look more prominent and altogether make a much more interesting photograph.

Taking close-up shots

Some caution is needed when taking close-up shots on deck. It's a common mistake to get too close, resulting in extreme distortion of anything near the lens. Some distortion is inevitable and acceptable, so find yourself a good position first. In this shot I lay along the coach roof and waited for the winch man to start trimming the headsail.

Always try to capture people actually working as this reduces their awareness of the camera and puts their muscles under tension, moving naturally and not looking limp and posed.

CARRIACOU
YACHT CLUB

- BAR
- SHOP
- LAUNDRY
- PHONE · FAX
TENNIS
DOCK

· RESTAURANT & BAR · DOCK ·
INTERNET CAFE · Shops · ↓

Local signs and menus are a great way of recalling the atmosphere of your trip.

Setting up close-up pictures

At one time a common problem was not being able to get close enough to the subject. Most digital cameras now have a macro button – this function replaces the need for close up lens attachments and generally has a flower symbol.

Auto focus can still be used in macro mode and this is particularly useful, but make sure you take the picture quickly as the smallest movement will take it out of focus.

Another time close-up shots prove useful is recording some local signs that, when you look at them back home, convey the atmosphere of the place you visited. In the left-hand picture this rickety sign for the local – excellent – yacht club gives you a great feel for the laid back approach to life in the Caribbean.

In the picture above a local menu says much about the great meal you had, framing this one to take in some of the wildly painted beach bar.

Zoom photography

Another exciting position for a photographer is sitting in between an advancing fleet, and it can produce some wonderful images. Here in my small dinghy I have positioned myself in the centre of the two advancing yachts with a long zoom lens left wide open – hoping that I fit between them!

This allows me sufficient sea room to make a decent exit should anyone get too close.

I focussed on the central group and allowed the nearer yachts to go out of focus. This leads the eye to the centre of the image, where most of the action is taking place. The sparkling diamond effect on the water is produced by the out of focus highlights.

Backlit pictures try very hard to become monochrome – the colour is washed out. Bright red always shows up in this setting and the prominent splashes of colour maintain its impact. When you use a long zoom lens it bunches the boats up, making the effect more dramatic.

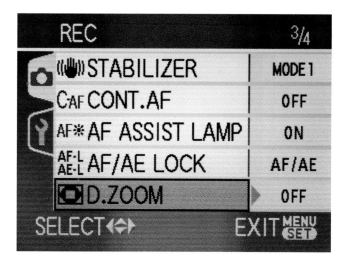

Digital zoom gets you closer than optical, but the quality will be slightly inferior. The option can be turned off.

Backlit scenes, where the sun is shining straight towards the lens, often confuses the metering system in cameras, producing too dark a picture. This function is again taken care of in iA.

A zoom lens allows you to effectively crop into a picture without getting too close and without losing quality.

Using the zoom function

Nowadays zoom lenses are of a comparable quality to fixed focal length ones and are standard fare on many compact cameras. This feature allows you to frame your subject without having to move yourself.

The zoom is immensely useful when photographing another yacht, as you have time to follow the subject and shoot at the best moment. A long zoom lens produces the same effect as a standard long lens by compressing the subject. The blue-hulled yacht oposite is around 50ft in length but looks smaller, until you count the crew.

By using a wide aperture you can pinpoint the focus to a chosen section of the yacht giving the people in the cockpit greater emphasis. An added feature on compact cameras is to bring into operation the digital zoom function. This can be useful in some cases but you will end up with degraded picture quality and also have difficulty in keeping the image in the frame.

Night photography

One aspect of night photography I really enjoy is firework displays. To get great results you need a display that has predominately coloured fireworks. Many these days are purely white and just look like streaks in the sky. The Dartmouth Regatta has two during its sailing week and are among the best I have seen.

The secret is a balanced time exposure, between the brightness of the land and the fireworks, so the use of a tripod is necessary. A trick I use is to have a piece of black card over the lens and quickly remove it when the firework goes off. This saves exposing the land detail – which is often brighter – while no fireworks are going off.

Believe it or not, this is a hand-held picture illuminated by the moon and some reflected light from a sun below the horizon! It really was quite dark but I wedged the camera against a post by the dinghy pontoon, set the camera to manual exposure and hoped for the best. Well, not quite but I was really surprised at how steady I could hold one of these small cameras and the sharpness of the picture and the delicate colour tones it produced.

There are various settings available in your camera. Automatic mode will ensure that exposure is correct.

This setting compensates for bright lights at night.

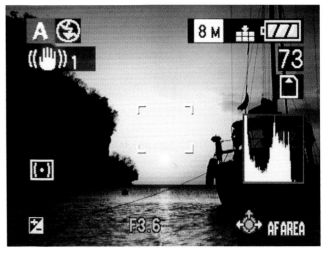

If you wish to be more adventurous with your pictures you can choose this option, called creative.

Some cameras have an option of sunset mode. In automatic mode the lighting is adjusted to create a successful picture.

Setting up good night photographs

The first thing to do is sit down and plan. Decide what you are going to shoot and the best angle. You might have been in this anchorage for a few days and, the night before, you noticed a magical opportunity when you went ashore to capture your yacht in a different light. Don't forget to take your tripod and a small torch. These will help you find the controls in the low light conditions.

Make sure you are familiar with how to set the delayed action control. This allows the camera to settle, removing the likelihood of camera shake. There is always a small vibration when you initially fire the shutter. This is not noticable in daylight conditions owing to the much higher shutter speed.

Low level light photography

A foggy morning at the marina berth meant I did not have to go far to find this image. The early morning light is diffused by the heavy mist which shows up as an eerie blue colour, fading out the yachts in the distance. It's awkward to get the exposure correct as the mist tends to be seen as being brighter than it really is.

Open up the aperture a stop to get some brightness and retain detail in the furthest yachts. I framed the shot to keep in the watery reflection, and the diminishing height of the masts leads your eye along the frame.

The forecast for the start of this Fastnet race was pretty grim but we ventured out in poor light and blustery conditions and I was able to grab this evocative shot of a pretty wooden yacht ploughing its way out of the Solent.

Sometimes when I bring my camera up from below into the colder air it takes a while to de-mist the lens and in this case I would have lost this shot. I had left my compact in a side open locker in its waterproof bag and it was therefore ready to go. The shot was taken on auto but I had to use +1 stop exposure compensation to keep it bright.

If you wish to experiment further there are various alternative settings to choose. This one is for night portraits.

Choose this setting for photographing general scenes at night or in very low light.

Low light photography

It's blowing a gale, raining cats and dogs, perhaps even snowing; not a day for photography, or is it? You might not shoot as many pictures as on a sunny day, but good photographs are still there to be had.

Almost invariably it will be overcast and the quality of light much poorer. Your meter, if set on auto, might have trouble coping and tend to stop down too much, making the pictures muddy. If you can, increase the exposure to keep the shots bright. If you don't have a splash-proof camera then some form of protection is needed – remember, oilskin pockets get wet as well. Keeping your camera dry should be easy enough with a plastic bag wrapped around it.

It's not often that you choose to go out in strong windy conditions, but if you are caught out or on a long passage then interesting seas can make for dramatic shots. Make sure you wear a safety harness if moving out of the cockpit.

Look for interesting shapes and wind effects on waves. Try to get some of your boat in the photograph, plus the helmsman steering if possible. If the tops of waves are being blown off, try to capture any light that is coming through the water to give the shot some depth and drama.

I have often returned home to find that the really rough conditions I experienced don't appear as extreme in my pictures.

Photography reduces everything to two dimensions and the drama can be lost. Including a person in the shot or perhaps another boat will give some scale to the waves, making them look more interesting.

Rain is an almost complete disaster when sailing, but when it's hammering down around you in a tranquil anchorage that is another matter. Heavy rain on water can produce droplets bouncing back up and can completely erase any horizon. Boats around you tend to become defused with the water vapour in the air, offering almost mystical pictures.

Fortunately snow will not be encountered often. Unfortunately it will confuse most metering systems. So, if in doubt, it might be best to bracket your exposures, i.e. take a range of exposures around the meter reading. Snow in the air whilst sailing will also confuse auto focussing lenses, trying to lock onto the flakes rather than the subject. To save your lens hunting around for something on which to lock, set it on manual if you can.

Some really nice shots can be had by wandering around moorings, at the water's edge and in boatyards. The colours of hulls and canvas covers seen in contrast with the snow create an explosion of colour.

Photographing landscapes

In north-west Canada we were known as the 'stick boat'; sailing rigs are quite unusual. Almost all vessels up north are motor boats capable of generating massive amounts of electricity, which suggests heating for my female crew. Nevertheless, even after a hard/cold day's sailing it can pay to clamber ashore – and capture the surroundings, especially if you are leaving the next morning and unlikely ever to return.

Rather than take a straight shot of the yacht, I included some foliage – in this case a dead tree – which contrasts wonderfully with the boat.

Make sure plenty of the anchorage background is showing. You know what it looked like but nobody else does, and this is a spectacular place.

The lighting in this shot was only available for a few moments as the sun was disappearing over the high tree line on the right. The sun was only shining on my yacht, giving it great emphasis.

Opportunities abound for pictures in harbours, not necessarily the modern marina but perhaps a stone-walled version that you enjoyed so much. Scenes and vantage points are all around and not just for shots of your boat. Local fishing boats with their nets etc all provide a rich environment for interesting pictures.

Look carefully around at the wealth of subjects and choose only the ones you would want to print at the end of the day. Carelessly shooting anything and every-thing means you stop looking for something really good. Everyone gets bored with meaningless pics. It is better to have 10 good ones than a 100 mediocre ones.

When you pay your harbour fees, have a look around. Often the office is high up and affords a good view. Take in the surroundings, and not just your boat, so that when you get home from your cruise the pictures will do the talking. Rolling hills in the background could easily be cut out if you just concentrate on close-ups of your berth. Take a few moments more and look at the visual possibilities around you that will make an ordinary photograph a bit different.

While still onboard, choose a point that looks as if it will make a good shooting position, taking into account the angle of the sun. If you have friends staying onboard, ask them to sit in the cockpit, doing something, maybe taking in the washing. Then head off to the spot you identified so that you can take pictures while the crew are not aware of the camera.

People in shots can add interest and you can send them copies when you get back home as a memento. Always look around for different angles; the one you spied from the boat might not be the best when you get onshore, so look around as you climb. When you find a suitable spot, and depending on your equipment, get some shots at a wide-angle setting to take in the whole scene. Include the whole anchorage and the hills beyond; don't worry that your boat is small in the frame. It will convey to those who see the pictures later a far better impression of your trip.

Now, gradually zoom in to the boat and get your friends enjoying themselves drinking your cold beer. A few shots midway on the zoom get in the feel of that water around you. If all the shots you have taken so far are in landscape mode, try turning the camera upright (portrait format). You might be surprised how different

The graphic icons show the options to get the best results. This screen is set on bright landscapes.

the picture becomes. The scene changes completely, almost making it another location.

In automatic mode the proper exposure and sharp focus will be taken care of, so you can concentrate on the composition.

Places onshore

Don't forget to take shots when you go ashore and to visit the town when you are away cruising. This adds an extra dimension to your story at the end of the year.

The culture of a new location is everywhere. Take pictures of the memorable restaurants and the food, the wonderful pile of shellfish, the local wine bottles, the menu on the wall outside. You might look out across the harbour to where you are moored. Include part of a building when framing your picture; this will give it depth rather than just another photograph of your boat.

Look at the buildings around you, coloured textured walls with flowers and creeper, close-ups, an unusual sign. These images are all around and it is easy to miss them.

Maybe there's a promise of a spectacular lighthouse on a rocky cliffside; make a trek to see if there are other places from which to shoot. In the example on the right I chose to cut off part of the lighthouse with the cliffside and include the rocky path, which leads your eye along it. The crew member gives some added interest and scale.

The inset shot from further back uses the crisp raking sunlight to its full advantage. Now the peeling paint is replaced by a strong silhouette, almost monochrome, and a dramatic statement is made.

Composing great photographs

At first glance you could be forgiven for thinking this an easy shot. But with 19.5 tons of classic yacht thundering towards you at 16 knots, an underinflated dinghy, a spluttering 4hp engine and the most nervous driver I have ever known, this definitely called for auto mode and some quick reactions as there was no way to keep pace with her.

Keeping in close had two benefits. I wanted this precise angle and manoeuvred the dinghy well upwind of her, and when she heeled a little more her boom end kissed the water – a headache or ducking would be on the cards for the less well prepared.

Framing – tips on how to do it better

Now for that magic moment. All is ready with your equipment and you look into the viewfinder. It's like entering another world and full concentration is necessary to capture the moment. It might be a few friends in the cockpit. If so, check their expressions; don't take the picture if you are not happy. Change your angle rather than giving them instructions, which will make them nervous. Don't stand at full height; bend your knees, sit down or look out through the companionway.

Make sure you are not cutting off someone's head or have something distracting in the shot like empty mugs or a half eaten sandwich. It might not be too obvious in the viewfinder but it will be later. Looking and seeing through the viewfinder is the difference between an ordinary and a great photograph.

You have to concentrate to see; the camera will only take what is there. Don't hope for luck or give only a quick glance prior to taking the shot. Ask yourself 'Is this really what I want?'

This screen enables you to review how your camera is currently set. In this case the shutter speed is a bit slow.

The screen here indicates that the shutter speed is even slower at 1/13. The shaking hand logo is a warning that there is a danger of the image being blurred.

Taking a tight entrance with only a foot of water below the keel is not always the best time to pick up the camera. But I liked the angle and colour of the rocky sides together with a sign that places the picture and an attractive yacht anchored in the background; this was not an opportunity to miss.

With little wind or current I swung the 44ft yacht abeam for a few seconds and, shooting on auto, grabbed a few frames before continuing the approach. I had to dial in an extra stop of exposure in compensation as the tendency with the very dark background would be to burn out the lighter areas.

Capturing the action in auto focus

Like most innovations auto focus took a while to catch on, but today it's a standard feature on all cameras. Canon's auto focus, launched in the early Nineties, was far superior to its predecessors and necessitated a complete system change for me.

Today it's still the best and gives me instantly sharp images which, for an action shot like this, are essential.

With the yacht and crew pushing to the limit, a big rolling sea and me wedged in the rolling flying bridge of the press boat I needed all the help I could get. Pictures like this are gone in a fraction of a second and auto focus allows me to use the camera with one hand.

Viewfinder or LCD monitor?

There are two ways to compose your digital photographs, through the LCD monitor or the viewfinder. At first it may seem that the monitor has the advantage because it displays a large and clear image. Normally I cannot see how you can successfully use just a monitor but in this case it proved its worth. The Canon G5 compact has a folding rear screen that can be tilted and still shows the image. For this shot I leaned over the side and held the camera close to the water, tilting the monitor up so that I could get this slightly unusual framing.

However, it does have some disadvantages. The ambient light will sometimes be so strong that it is difficult to see what is on the screen. In this case you can resort to the viewfinder and might find that you prefer it.

For any kind of action shots a viewfinder is essential as you can then concentrate on just the image and not what is going on around the camera. Often there is information about exposure and focus which saves you having to look back at the monitor.

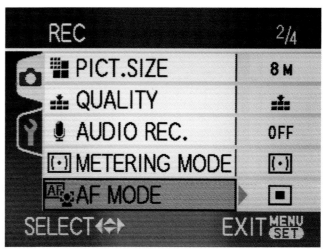

This screen indicates that this camera is set in auto focus mode.

The information on this screen indicates that the camera is set in program mode. The flash is turned off. The image will be 8 megabytes in size. The battery charge level is shown. The shaking hand logo indicates that stabilising is set to operate continuously. The lower right icon is an auto focus selection setting. The lower left icons indicate that the camera has measured the exposure from the whole area of the screen, and that exposure compensation has been set.

The importance of light, colour and exposure

Light is one element of the picture over which you have very little control but you can use it to good effect by choosing angles that give your shots life. Here I positioned myself so that the light is almost shining back into the lens. The contrast from one side of the hulls to the other and the translucent effect on the sails really gives this picture great presence.

Exposure is critical as it is easy to fool the meter into getting it too dark because of the amount of light falling on the camera's sensor. About two thirds of a stop extra should do it; any more and it will start to get washed out.

Colour is compromised, sometimes almost becoming monochrome, but usually someone is wearing something red and this gives the picture more depth.

In this shot I experimented with an angled horizon which amplifies the impact of the heeled yachts.

Light is all around us, but it is critical to choose your angle carefully as it makes a dramatic difference to the end result.

For instance taking the shot above, I decided to frame the division of sand and sky in unequal proportions using a wide angle lens to give a sense of the vast beach area. The golden sand contrasts with the blue of the sky but to give some sort of scale I included the figure with an orange top placed slightly off centre. Orange is the opposite colour to blue on the colour scale, making for

a striking contrast against the deep blue sky. The raking sunlight from the right brought out the ripple effect on the sand as well as giving light and shade to the figure.

If I had shot further to the right with the sun behind me, there would have been no shadows, the light would have been flat and the colours less intense due to the lack of contrast.

To get the very best sailing shot it is better not to have the sun directly behind you. Although you will

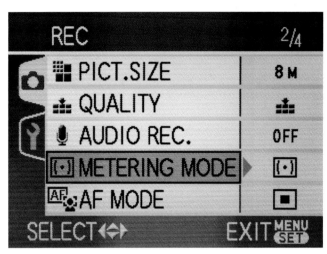

Select your metering mode with care so that it is appropriate to the subject you wish to photograph.

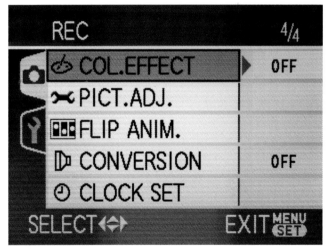

You may wish to experiment with the different colour effects that are offered by your camera, for instance black and white and sepia.

get the best colour rendition, you won't get any shadows. However, if you place yourself with the sun to your side, roughly in line with your shoulders at an angle of between 45–135 degrees, you will still get good colour but the shadows formed will give your picture more shape and definition. Once the sun is any further in front of 45 degrees to your shoulders you will be looking into the light source – a good picture can still be taken but the colour quality will deteriorate and you may suffer reflections in the lens.

Also, remember to never point your camera directly at the sun, as you could damage the sensor as well your eyes!

When and how to use flash

Nowadays all compact cameras come with some form of flash. These built in flashes are not that powerful compared with flashguns you attach and are only really suitable to cover distances up to 3m (10ft). The one advantage is that they are always ready to use.

In this picture the flash allowed me to bring out detail in the people and balance the available light of the scenery. If I had not used flash the people would have been dark shapes or the scenery would have burnt out.

Flash was essential for this shot in a boat shed which had several different light sources. In the background are fluorescent lights and some skylights. In the foreground is another skylight providing a shaft of light on the foredeck and some general available light from the shed entrance behind me.

Selecting your scene in portrait mode and choosing the outdoor option allows the meter to determine the exposure for the available light.

This option allows you to balance your flash, mainly used to reduce the power in order not to over-light your subject.

The symbol with the arrow facing down indicates that the red eye reduction facility is operational.

This setting allows you to choose the flash mode appropriate to your subject.

Automatic flash

A camera's flash metering system, however intelligent, does not always get it right.

I lit the man on the foredeck (opposite) with the camera's flash after taking a general meter reading of the available light with the camera's meter. I adjusted the camera's exposure compensation by minus one stop and used the flash on full power, bringing emphasis on to the workman.

This created a pleasing natural balance to the eye whilst keeping the attention on the main part of the subject.

Some cameras have the option of reducing the flash power; this is called 'fill-in flash', as used in the picture on p62–3. This lets you control the amount of light fired, preventing the subject from being over lit.

Other options are 'full power' (as the name suggests) and yet another is 'red eye' – usually a burst of flashes before the main flash to reduce the pupil size. Red eye is the reflection of the flash off the back of the eye and the only sure way to eliminate it is to have the flashgun at a greater angle from the camera lens. This is not usually possible with compact cameras.

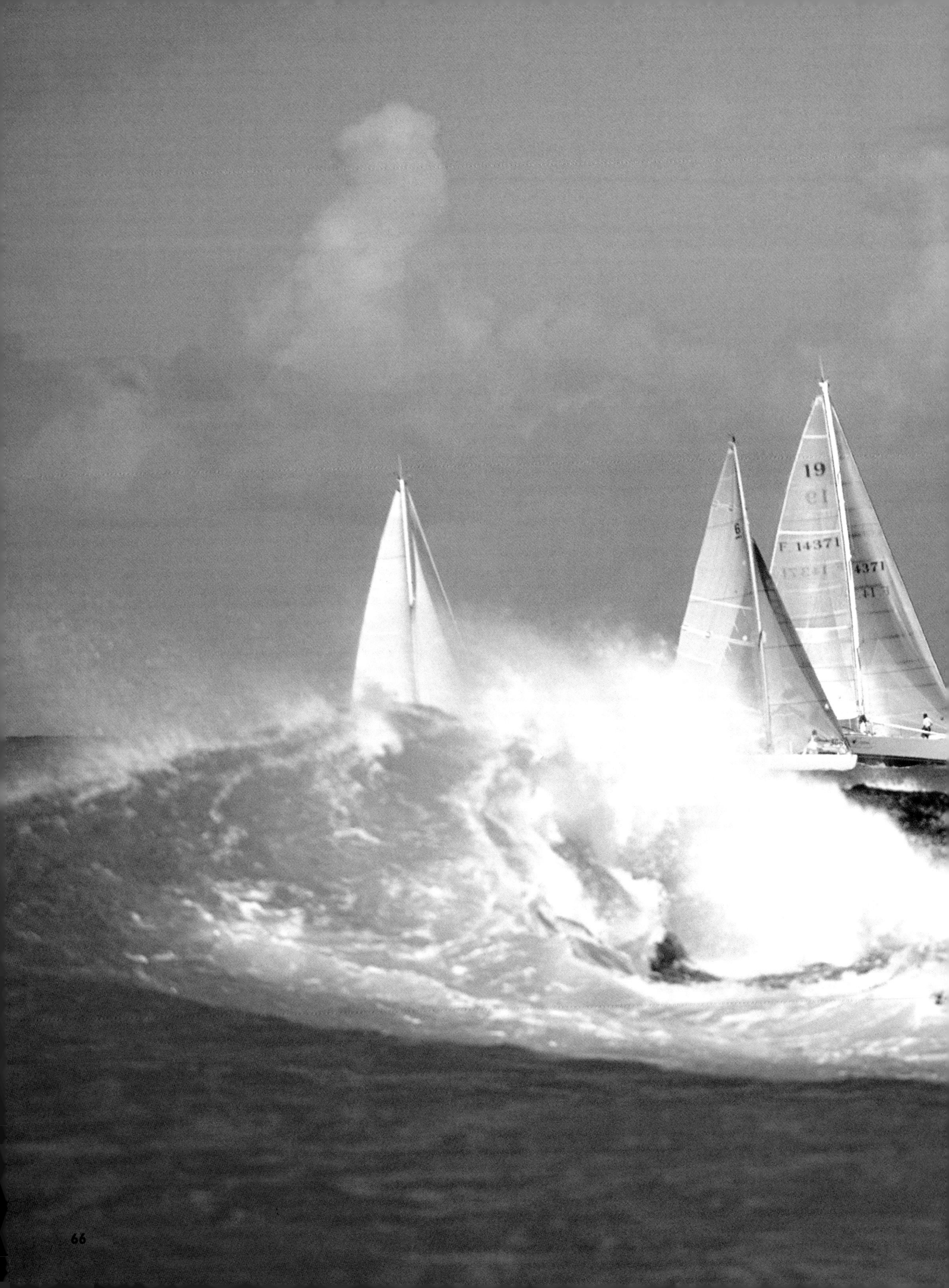
19
F 14371
4371

Custom settings

Sometimes you need to override a camera's automatic settings. I waited for some time for a group of yachts to position themselves behind the rocks where the ocean swell was crashing. It gave me time to compose the shot and, having decided that I wanted the yachts to be sharp and that the white surf would affect the auto setting adversely, I switched off the auto focus function and manually set the distance to infinity.

The metering would normally have read the large amount of white in the centre of the picture and produced too dark a result, so I set the exposure compensation to plus 1 stop to keep an overall good colour balance. Most compact cameras have these controls and it is a standard feature on SLRs.

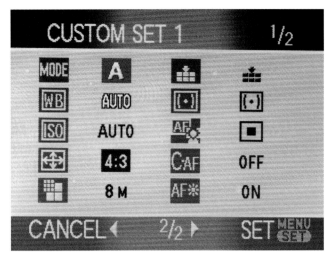

When you take your pictures you can set up all the parameters that you prefer your camera to use. These can be set either to run at start up or can be used for your favourite shooting mode.

Controls on SLR cameras are more sophisticated, especially the lens control. The option settings shown are for focussing and image stabilisation. Note both are easily accessible.

Creating your own settings

The camera I use is a Canon EOS SLR. It's comparable with less expensive digital cameras because in many ways it has the same controls. Most of what I suggest in this section can be applied to a smaller digital camera.

The big difference between my large Canon camera and lenses compared with a compact camera is mainly its speed of use and the quality of the lenses. By speed I mean not only operating the controls but also its ability to write the information almost instantly to the memory card. It's now possible to shoot frame after frame without the process being interrupted. It was the case until recently that I would have to wait for the camera's temporary memory buffer to catch up writing to the card. Now, with compatible camera electronics and high speed cards, this has almost been eliminated. Even sports photographers who need to shoot continuous bursts at 10 frames per second will not now miss the action.

So the compacts are catching up fast. Don't be fooled by the amount of megapixels – it's really the quality of the pixels that are transmitted that counts.

With the advance in camera electronics more and more options can be found with each new model. One particularly useful option is the ability to set a group of parameters, with which you can start up your camera. For instance you may want to start up the camera in wide angle, in program mode with a certain ISO etc.

These can all be set and recalled by accessing one custom set from your menu. Some cameras offer several sets, useful when going between different subjects.

Using custom settings

The picture opposite required some careful adjustment of settings on the camera so that I could fully concentrate on shooting the yacht when it came into range. There is a strong background light to contend with, as well as reflections off the water, so a degree of exposure compensation was set to retain brightness in the predominately backlit picture.

As there is plenty of light a lower/slower ISO setting was used, which resulted in better colour quality. (This is comparable to slower film over a higher speed film which gives a grainy effect.) The sea was lumpy so I decided to go for a higher speed over depth of focus – this places the emphasis squarely on the yacht, with the background fading out.

The reflection of the red part of the spinnaker on the water is essential to lift the otherwise monochrome effect.

It's not always necessary to take full height shots of sailing boats. Try shooting with the mast half cut off, revealing more of the deck. Alternatively you can frame up close on the cockpit or the bow, hopefully with some dramatic waves rolling around it.

Manual exposure

From time to time the unexpected happens and in this picture the sun had broken through the clouds and cast a narrow strip of light across the two yachts. Enhancing the image, the sun was backlighting the spinnakers but this combination would have defeated most camera metering systems.

By switching to manual mode and changing the metering to spot mode, I concentrated on the centre of the viewfinder, where spot metering works. I focussed on the bright strip of light and took the reading. I could then re-frame the subject to compose the shot without the need to keep checking the exposure. Exposing for the highlight makes the darker areas even darker, adding to the dramatic effect.

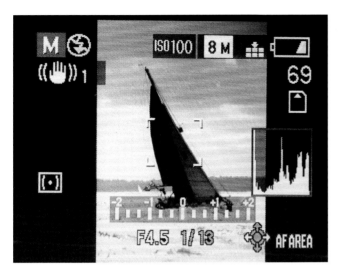

You can display lots of information on your monitor screen.

Or switch some or all of it off to have an uninterrupted view.

Manual exposure settings

Built-in metering has to contend with a wide range of situations. The end result can sometimes fail and this depends on the competence of the system. The meter is actually trying to find an average point of colour and density in your composition. This relates to a set standard reflectance value of 18% shade of grey, which was selected by Kodak many years ago. This then translates into an exposure that produces a well balanced picture for a normal subject. However, it can go wrong when the spectrum of the shot is limited. When you photograph a pure white piece of card it comes out grey; this is because there are no other references available to the meter, only white. The result is under-exposure so by opening up the lens a stop or two you will get the correct colour value. This could quite easily happen on a very dull day when everything already looks grey. By opening up the aperture you allow more light to record the image correctly and the resulting photographs have more vibrancy.

Conversely, a black card would come out too light when photographed. How often have you taken shots with flash of people in dark jackets to find their faces

are burnt out – too light? In this situation, if your camera allows, stop down the lens a half to one stop and the results will be more pleasing.

Most digital cameras use meter readings taken from many points over the frame; this is known as evaluative metering. Information is gathered from as many as fifty different places to compute the exposure. Usually this is the best type to use but if you have extremely bright edges to your picture, like sky or clouds, these can adversely affect the end result and produce an under-exposed picture. To counter this try selecting a different metering option. Most cameras have three included, the other two being centre weighted and spot metering. You can see the one selected on your screen by the different icons. Spot metering takes a reading for the small central part of the screen while centre weighted takes a reading from a bigger central part – this is probably the best to use when you have very bright edges. The only reliable way to obtain an exact reading is with a hand-held exposure meter, but this item is probably not going to make it into too many camera bags.

Coming home one day in a fair breeze and a short Solent chop, I noticed this pretty Contessa powering along. The sun was low and ahead. I was looking for a striking image. This angle was perfect as the light through the tan sails produced some lovely shapes together with the very sparkly backlit water.

Metering this type of subject is quite difficult as I had extremes of shadow and highlight. I actually switched to manual mode and took a reading from the sky. The uniform grey cloud gave me an average reading which formed the basis of the final exposure.

Manual focus

This picture resulted from a commission to shoot the left-hand white yacht in a variety of good sailing conditions during a race for the company sponsor. One of the classic mistakes when using auto focus is to forget to check that the subject is in the centre of the frame. How many times do you see a picture of two people, heads off-centre and blurred, with brilliantly lit sharp wallpaper 20ft (6m) behind them?

The same applies to this situation; I wanted to focus on just one yacht. By turning the camera/lens onto manual focus you can ensure that your picture is sharp where you want it to be. The effect will be more pronounced with a long lens as the focus is more concentrated. If you have image stabilisation make sure this option is turned on to avoid camera shake.

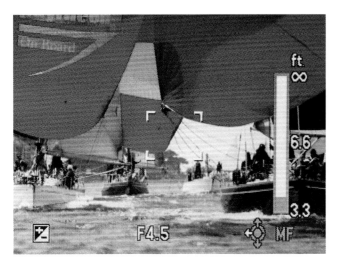

The primary information here is for manual focussing. If you use the setting shown here, the shot will be out of focus as the scale on the right indicates that the lens is focussed at a distance of just over 3.3ft.

Accurate focussing is very important for the special picture that you don't want to lose.

The importance of choice when focussing

In order to have an acceptable picture the main subject must be in focus. This might seem obvious and in most viewfinders the subject can appear sharp but, in fact, it is easy to lose concentration just prior to taking your picture. If the main part of your subject is off-centre, the focussing area that your camera uses is defined in the centre of the viewfinder. This is usually shown by some angled brackets. Arrange these over your main subject and then focus. You will then be able to re-frame your picture while keeping the focus at that distance. This ensures that the main element in your shot is sharp. For instance it is often better when taking portraits to allow the background to become very soft as it avoids distracting details that are not required. This ensures that the main element in your shot is sharp.

If the camera is in auto focus mode the technique is to hold the shutter button half way down to lock the focus at that distance, and then re-frame as before.

Focussing can have a great impact on the end result. If you are using a long lens, focussing is more critical because the depth of sharpness is greatly reduced, but you can pick out a section of a boat and make it pin-sharp. Or with a wide angle lens the whole image can easily be in focus.

Objects nearer the lens can sometimes be kept out of focus to enhance the composition by leading your eye further into the picture.

Using filters

It pays to have your camera always ready to go when the unexpected happens. Here the weather conditions were pretty dull, as can be seen from the background, but the occasional shafts of sunlight kept appearing. I followed one along and it lit up this beautiful classic yacht. The stunning whites of the sails and hull contrast sharply with the blackish background, giving the picture an almost 3D appearance.

I let the background go dark as my priority was to keep the yacht sparkling white but retain detail in the sails.

SLR cameras are easily fitted with filters, but compact cameras do not often have this facility.

The value of filters

The graduated filter is useful from time to time but the effects are easily overdone. Unlike conventional screw-in filters the graduated types are supplied as flat sheets with their own lens mount. This allows the filter to be moved up and down for accurate positioning.

The neutral density type graduate the colours that are there, giving the greatest density at the darkest part. They come in various degrees of graduation usually specified in stops, eg 1 stop grad, 2 stop etc. This means that the top of the filter allows 2 stops less of light than the bottom. For instance, when photographing a landscape, if you have a very bright sky with a darkish foreground a graduated filter will stop some of the bright light registering at the top, allowing more detail to show, while letting more light into the bottom half, which would otherwise have been darker. This balances the contrast and overall result.

The colour graduation type, as the name suggests, comes in a variety of colours and works in the same way as neutral density filters but graduates colour as well over the picture. The colour produced will often look stronger on your print than when you see it through the viewfinder, so use sparingly.

Contentious issues abound here. The manufacturers' lists of effect filters are long and varied. Some are useful; others are purely gimmicks. I personally don't enjoy using them, and you will rarely find one in my

For this picture I used a one stop graduation filter to slightly darken the sky and bring out the subtle blue and pink tones that would otherwise be lost. On an SLR camera this is easy to position and to see the effect in the viewfinder. It's a different matter on a compact as you really have to hold the filter with one hand and experiment. Many compact cameras now feature a live view monitor which gives you almost the same control as an SLR camera, but some are a little slow in refreshing the screen during movement.

camera bag. There have been times when a job called for a particular effect, but I have rarely seen them used well and more often misused. If you are tempted to use this sort of filter use it with a purpose, not just as an excuse to enhance the image content.

Other types of filter commonly used are **Skylights** – more to protect the front element of the lens –

although it's not always possible to fit them to compacts. These can be useful if you get a lot of spray on the lens, as the salt water may leave hairline scratch marks which build up over time. This filter can be quickly cleaned and cheaply replaced.

Polarising filters are used to cut down reflections, allowing you to see through water, remove partial reflections which intensify colour saturation and darken a blue sky dramatically – use the sky part in moderation as the effect often tends to look overdone. Rotate the front element of the filter and you will see the effect on your image as it changes between dark and light. Make sure you buy the circular type and not the cheaper linear type which can stop the auto focus and metering systems from functioning.

Supplementary lenses

If you happen to be sailing on an 80ft Swan in perfect sailing conditions, you obviously have a wide choice of subjects. However, wherever you are look around and plan not only your shots/angles but the lens that will give you the best results. This is more difficult to do with compact cameras but some now have the option of wide and long lens attachments. These attach to the front element of the lens on your camera.

For this shot I positioned the empty winch in the foreground; it was too obvious to go close to the pretty girl but she still plays a central role in the framing. I waited for the yacht to heel. Light was raking across the deck, producing some interesting long shadows and keeping some of the rich blue sea, which gave it that full touch of luxury.

SLR cameras support a wide range of interchangeable lenses. Compact cameras are limited to supplementary lenses that can only be attached to the existing lens.

How to get better pictures by changing the lens

A typical 35mm SLR outfit could contain many lenses; these will range from fixed focal length lenses to zooms.

- **Ultra wide angle lenses** of around 17mm focal length are great for photographing interiors and deck shots, where there is limited space to get back from your subject. Your sharpness range available is generally everything you can see.
- **Wide angle lenses** range around 24 to 28mm focal length. Again, most of what you see is sharp and they tend to give you less distortion on objects near to the lens.
- **Standard lenses** are typically in the order of 50mm. These produce an angle of view similar to that seen by the naked eye. Focussing now becomes slightly more critical.
- **Short telephoto lenses** range between 100–200mm and start to get a little bigger and heavier. They're good for taking portraits, as you don't need to get so close to fill the frame. Focussing is more critical than for standard lenses.
- **Long telephoto lenses** range from 300mm to 1200mm. The shorter ones can be hand-held whereas the longer ones require a tripod. Focus now is ultra critical. These lenses are used mainly for sports and wildlife photography.
- **Zoom lenses** are every bit as good as their fixed focal length counterparts nowadays. They come in a wide variety of lengths from wide angle to telephoto versions. Their usefulness lies in their ability to span several focal lengths with one lens. Physically, they are larger and heavier but their usefulness definitely outweighs this disadvantage. Many now come with image stabilisation built in.

- **Specialist lenses**. One of my favourite specialist lenses is the 500mm mirror lens. This offers a compact design, of reasonable weight and short length. It produces unusual shaped highlights in the out-of-focus areas but comes with a fixed aperture, usually of f8.

Classic yachts offer unlimited potential for any creative photographer. Here I wanted to capture the beautiful shape of the curving leeward topsides and the sense of utter concentration from the many crew needed to sail one of these ladies from a past era. The angle of the mainsheet straining through those hand-made wooden blocks and the clean wake at 15 knots all add to the drama of this shot.

White balance

A new phrase has crept into our lives with digital photography, white balance, a term uncommon only a few years back but now an essential one and not difficult to understand. To get the very best results you need to remember that all light has a certain colour, eg daylight is a bluish light while, indoors, a normal household bulb is an orange colour. If the whites in your picture are to stay white then the correct white balance setting must be used. Today this is a simple procedure compared with the era of film which either had a specific colour temperature or required the use of special filters.

The WB setting can usually be left on its auto setting – AWB is a common symbol. But if you set it manually – usually choosing one of the graphic symbols – you get a more precise result.

You will notice in this picture of a Greek monastery that even the shadow area of its walls has a slight colour cast. The intense sunlight was so blue that even setting the WB to daylight was not quite enough.

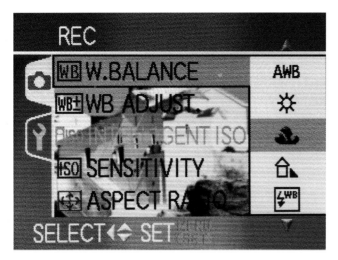

White balance can be set to automatic or, for optimum results, it can be set manually by choosing the icon to match the conditions.

In this case the exposure compensation is set to + 2/3rds of a stop to retain the brilliance of the white building.

What is white balance?

White balance is the process of removing unrealistic colour casts, so that objects which appear white are rendered white in your photo. Proper camera white balance has to take into account the colour temperature of a light source, which refers to the relative warmth or coolness of white light. Our eyes are very good at judging what is white under different light sources; however, digital cameras can have great difficulty with auto white balance (AWB). An incorrect WB can create unsightly blue, orange, or even green colour casts, which are unrealistic and particularly damaging to portraits. Understanding digital white balance can help you avoid colour casts created by your camera's AWB, therefore improving your photographs under a wide range of lighting conditions.

The following table is a guide to colour temperatures expressed in degrees Kelvin for some common light sources:

Colour temp	Light source
1000–2000 K	Candlelight
2500–3500 K	Tungsten bulb (household variety)
3000–4000 K	Sunrise/sunset (clear sky)
4000–5000 K	Fluorescent lamp
5000–5500 K	Electronic flash
5000–6500 K	Daylight with clear sky (sun overhead)
6500–8000 K	Moderately overcast sky
9000–10000 K	Shade or heavily overcast sky

The white balances listed previously are in order of increasing colour temperature. However, many compact cameras do not include a 'shade' white balance, although some cameras do include a 'Fluorescent H' setting, which is designed to work in newer daylight-calibrated fluorescents.

Fortunately, all digital cameras contain a variety of preset white balances, making it easy for you to set against their graphic icon. In tricky lighting situations you can set your own custom white balance, by taking a picture of a white reference, and then set that as the white balance for future photos under the same lighting conditions.

The descriptions for the above white balances are just rough estimates for the actual lighting under which they work best. In fact, cloudy could be used in place of daylight depending on the time of day, elevation, or degree of haziness. In general, if your image appears too cool on your LCD screen preview (regardless of the setting), you can quickly increase the colour temperature by selecting the appropriate symbol on your camera. If the image is still too cool (or warm if going in the other direction) you can resort to manually entering a colour temperature actually in the Kelvin setting in your camera's menu.

If all else fails and the image still does not have the correct WB after inspecting it on a computer, you can adjust the colour balance to remove additional colour casts with programs such as Photoshop, but you are then degrading the quality of the image.

Waiting for a firework display to start, I wandered around the massive harbour in Las Palmas and this assortment of local boats caught my eye. Their pontoon lit by one street lamp from the road, with the ARC fleet in the background, had the makings of a shot worth trying for. I wondered if I should use my small tripod, but this did not go high enough, so I needed to hand-hold the camera. I set the ISO to 1600 – a high setting – and fully opened the aperture to f2.8. The reading gave me a 1/20 of a second exposure, the maximum I could achieve. I set the white balance to cloudy daylight and not to tungsten to retain the orange glow, otherwise the whites would have been bright white and would have ruined the warm effect I wanted to achieve.

Fortunately there was little or no movement in the water so I took a deep breath and pressed the shutter.

Histograms

This was a rough day on the water with low cloud, rain and a definite icy chill. These are not the ideal starting points for a day's work. If you are positive, however, something will happen.

In this shot, with heavy rain and everyone tucked up in foul weather gear, I am not sure who was more surprised when this boat appeared from out of the murk on the Scottish loch.

With the meter going haywire I manually set an exposure 1.5 stops less than indicated to keep the picture bright. Keeping the aperture wide open to get the maximum shutter speed possible to try to freeze some of the spray that was flying around, a great sequence of frames transpired. Not the ideal promotional shot for the sponsor, but the crew loved them.

What are histograms?

Understanding image histograms is an important factor when working with pictures from a digital camera. A histogram can tell you whether or not your image will be properly exposed, whether the lighting is harsh or flat. If you keep an eye on histograms you will gradually build up a knowledge of what makes a good balanced picture and improve your technique as a photographer. Each pixel in an image has a colour which has been produced by some combination of the primary colours red, green, and blue (RGB). Each of these colours can have a brightness value ranging from 0 to 255 for a digital image.

The region where most of the brightness values are present is called the tonal range. Tonal range can vary drastically from image to image. There is no ideal histogram which all images should try to mimic; histograms should merely be representative of the tonal range in the scene and what the photographer wishes to convey.

Although most cameras will produce midtone histograms when in an automatic exposure mode, the distribution of peaks within a histogram also depends on the tonal range of the subject matter. Images where most of the tones occur in the shadows are called low key, whereas with high key images most of the tones are in the highlights.

The histogram read-out is an option that can be displayed. This is a typical example indicating that the shot is well balanced.

Going for a sundowner after a gruelling day's sailing in the Caribbean, it is easy to forget to take along your camera. Inevitably some magic scene will appear in the form of another dramatic sunset. In this shot I have deliberately kept in some foreground as the angles of the pontoon and the palm fronds give the picture a Caribbean flavour.

Before the photograph has been taken, it is useful to assess whether or not your subject matter qualifies as high or low key. Since cameras measure reflected as opposed to incident light, they are unable to assess the absolute brightness of their subjects. Many cameras contain sophisticated algorithms which try to circumvent this limitation, and estimate how bright an image should be. These estimates frequently result in an image where the average brightness is placed in the midtones. This is usually acceptable; however, high and low key scenes frequently require the photographer to manually adjust the exposure, relative to what the camera will do automatically. A good rule-of-thumb is that you will need to manually adjust the exposure whenever you want the average brightness in your image to appear brighter or darker than the midtones.

Most digital cameras are better at reproducing low key scenes since they prevent any region from becoming so bright that it turns into solid white, regardless of how dark the rest of the image might become as a result. High key scenes, on the other hand, often produce images which are significantly under-exposed. Fortunately, under-exposure is usually more forgiving than over-exposure. Detail can never be recovered when a region becomes so over-exposed that it becomes solid white. When this occurs the highlights are said to be clipped.

A histogram can also describe the amount of contrast. Contrast is a measure of the difference in brightness between light and dark areas in a scene. Broad histograms reflect a scene with significant contrast, whereas narrow histograms reflect less contrast and may appear flat or dull. This can be caused by any combination of subject matter and lighting conditions. Photos taken in the fog will have low contrast, while those taken under strong daylight will have higher contrast.

Contrast can have a significant visual impact on an image by emphasising texture. Contrast can also vary for different regions within the same image owing to both subject matter and lighting.

ISO and why it matters

For action/fast moving subjects the primary objective is to get them sharp. Sometimes there might not be enough light or you just want to ensure you have a fast enough shutter speed to catch all that spray. The option is to select a higher ISO speed. If 200 is your normal then 400 will give you an extra stop's worth of shutter speed. There is a small premium to pay in that you reduce picture and colour quality.

In this picture I was aiming to get the boat backlit by the sparkling sea, manually metering the area first, to make sure of a consistent exposure balance as the light changed. I also needed to keep the sea bright and retain shadow detail on the side of the motor boat.

ISO explained

Sometimes you will see references to ASA/ISO; the ASA (American Standards Association) and ISO (International Standards Organisation) are basically the same thing. They relate in digital/sensor terms to the sensitivity (speed) of a particular sensor setting to light and usually to image colour quality and apparent sharpness as well.

A low ISO number, say 50, means that it takes more light (shutter open longer or aperture wider) to properly expose your digital image but you get better colour tones and sharpness as there is far more information in the final image. You would therefore be able to enlarge it more than a higher sensor setting and produce better looking prints.

A higher number means it takes less time. Say you have ISO 100 speed rating and the proper exposure for that situation is 1/500 of a second at an aperture of f16. If you switched to an ISO 200 setting it would be 1/1000 of a second at f16. Conversely if you had a setting rated at ISO 50 you would set your shutter to 1/250 at f16.

Fast speeds are useful for capturing subjects in low light or high speed or when you can't use a tripod, like the picture of the motor boat on p94/95 where I wanted to keep sharpness in the flying spray and needed a 1/1000 of a second minimum to do this. Night photography is another time to use a higher ISO setting, particularly if there is any movement such as in water that you want sharp.

This picture of fishing boats on a beach is the other extreme to the power boat picture on pages 94–5. Here, there is very bright light, vivid colours and a mostly stationary subject. To get the best out of a scene like this, the ISO should be set manually to its slowest setting, usually 50. The sensor will then produce the maximum detail in the range of tones between various colours. As the sky was cloudless I framed the tree over it to bring the eye down to the fishing boats; this gives the effect of looking between them out onto the brilliant blue sea. This had the detrimental effect of introducing a large dark area that the meter would confuse into making the final result too light. I got around it by taking the reading manually around the stern/beach area to retain detail and colour in the highlights.

For this fast moving subject the panning mode scene was selected and the image stabilisation setting turned off in order to retain the feeling of speed over the water.

The ISO setting relates to sensor/film sensitivity; the lower the number the slower is the sensitivity but the lower numbers provide better colour rendition.

Boat to boat photography

If your friends ask you to photograph their boat, try thinking of an original way to shoot it. Start off with the standard shot of the whole boat side, but also give some thought to different angles and the conditions of the day. Look for the best points, perhaps the available lighting or, as here, the large swell going across the frame.

Each shot will present you with opportunities so take advantage and produce a series of different pictures that your friends would be proud to own. They can return the compliment, but not at the same time – there is nothing worse than having photographers pointing their cameras at you!

You may never find yourself in the middle of a racing fleet but this picture illustrates the use of background elements that can add an extra dimension to your pictures. Here another yacht is crossing ahead of the boat I am photographing but by positioning myself on the leeward quarter, the other boat's mainsail makes a distinctly unusual backdrop. I was shooting on a long lens to foreshorten the distance between the two yachts, creating a little more drama, along with the heel of the white yacht. Again, the picture is tightly cropped to keep your attention on the main subject and not include distracting backgrounds.

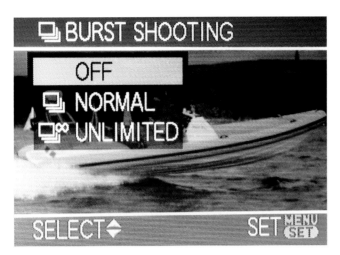

For high speed shots it is handy to use burst shooting which is motor drive by another name.

This subject will be close to many an owner's heart. If I had a pound for every time I have heard a skipper despair at not having a photographic record of that brilliant sail I would be writing this book on my own Caribbean island.

Understandably, when your boat is singing along under a brisk breeze or crashing through a wall of water you cannot just offload into the dinghy. However, as with all problems, there is a solution. It will depend on the competence of others and their willingness to help. One answer is to link up with a friend who wants to do some photography.

Arranging to go for a day's sail together allows the opportunity for both to obtain a result. It's best to choose your moment carefully, when weather conditions are good. Sunshine makes all the difference to a photograph and it's worth waiting for the right conditions.

There is no doubt that, when it comes to photographing boats, the job is made slightly easier if your craft happens to be propelled by a 200hp engine: there is nothing like instant manœuvrability when it comes to freedom of creativity. Sailing yachts, however, are severely restricted, particularly if flying spinnakers or cruising chutes. If this is your type of vessel some careful planning is needed. The following guidelines can be adapted for both:

1. Whatever your boat, take care to keep a good look out for other craft AT ALL TIMES. It is all too easy to become absorbed in what you are doing at the expense of others.

2. Before setting off, plan for one long leg between two known points. Providing the wind is neither too light

nor too strong try to start with a fine reach, a point of sail that shows a sailing yacht at its best.

3. Take into account lighting conditions. If it's mid-summer do not attempt to photograph around lunchtime; the sun will be high in the sky and will produce a very flat result. Ideally, aim for a degree of shadow or cross-lighting to add interest. Look at your subject, try to enhance its shape and add drama. Experiment with shooting into the sun, getting an intensity of light behind the sails.

4. Never rely on a helmsman to take photographs; he will have quite enough on his plate if he is to avoid a collision. Place your chosen photographer onboard the camera boat, making sure there are adequate supplies of memory in the camera. In an ideal world he would use a short telephoto or zoom lens (70–200mm). A shorter focal length lens would require the boats being too close for safety or result in an image not big enough to fill the frame.

5. I find that standing or crouching is better than sitting down. Your legs act as natural shock absorbers and reduce vibrations from the boat's motion. When sitting down this motion is transmitted through your body and your arms, contributing to camera shake.

6. The best starting position for a camera is ahead and to leeward, which allows the subject to pass slowly to weather. If the camera boat has adequate power to keep up with its subject it should then go around the subject's stern and overtake. This manœuvre should be carried out slowly, leaving the photographer to look through the viewfinder for the best bow wave, angle of heel, reflections etc – all those little extras that make an ordinary picture something special.

7. When you are satisfied that you have your pictures, change direction and return to the starting point. Remember, KEEP SHOOTING. Lighting and sea conditions change constantly. Change over and start again. (If the leg is long enough, swap over halfway.) Alternatively, you can use a dinghy. But be careful when standing up. If the dinghy is fast enough to keep up, your subject can be positioned anywhere. However, most small dinghies are unlikely to have the necessary speed. This being the case, the subject needs to sail past at a given distance, slow down until the dinghy has repositioned itself and repeat the procedure.

A photographer in a small craft should always wear a lifejacket/buoyancy aid. Dinghies are unstable and, when at sea, unpredictable wash and bigger waves add an extra dimension. If possible, a second person should be onboard, leaving the photographer free to concentrate on the job and keep the camera (and bag) dry.

Stabilising your camera

We were in the teeth of a gale and the sun was setting; there was not much time to capture these yachts heading back across the Channel from the delightful harbour of Treguier in northern France.

With increasing amounts of water coming over us it was hard to make headway and I needed as much help that evening as the camera could muster. This is where image stabilisation really comes into play. Clever wizardry inside the camera or sometimes the lens itself helps to eliminate vibrations equivalent to some manufacturers' claims of 2–3 stops. Stabilisation is now a common function on many cameras, often as a default. You can turn it on but be aware it will use a bit more battery power.

There are two modes for image stabilisation. One tries to eliminate vibration in vertical and horizontal planes, the other only in the vertical plane, allowing you to pan a shot, leaving the horizon to blur.

The jitter/movement screen is a test by the camera to detect unwanted movement. The icons show a neutral situation.

Preventing camera shake

Always use both hands to hold a digital camera on a zoom lens setting or this could promote camera shake. A great deal of care is required when you press the shutter; it does not need more than a delicate press. I have watched some people taking photographs, and the effort involved in pressing that little button not only generates violent shake but can also move the camera downwards, resulting in a good collection of feet pictures; you know the problem!

Only use enough pressure to move the button. Many cameras operate the focussing and exposure when it is

half depressed, so feel for when this happens, check the subject and follow through smoothly. If you are photographing a busy subject, perhaps from a motor boat, it's a common mistake to brace yourself against something solid. Remember this will also be vibrating and can add to the vibration you are actually trying to eliminate.

One useful tip in determining the slowest shutter speed to use for a given focal length lens is to choose a speed no slower than the focal length of the lens – the longest one being for a zoom. So a 200mm lens could be held

at 1/250. Take into account your IS system, some of which claim to give an extra 3–4 stops of speed and you could be down 1/30 or 1/15 second. Personally, I would keep to 1/250 with IS on for the crispest image. However, as most SLR sensors are not equivalent to the full frame of a 35mm camera, from where the focal length is originally calculated, they more usually correspond to about +1.6. Therefore you must apply this factor to the focal length of your lens. This might explain why on most compact cameras, the focal length is shown against an equivalent for a full frame 35mm.

With an ocean swell and vast stern waves coming off these J Class yachts, it would be too easy to get camera shake. It is sad to think that when you return, what should be dynamic photos are reduced to fuzzy blurs. Make sure the IS setting is turned on; as both you and your subject are moving, you need speed to keep it all sharp. Until the advent of IS the best piece of advice I ever had was to bend my knees and float my body, rather like the suspension of a car.

Panning shots joined together

I had a day off in the delightful setting of the Morlaix estuary but I still kept a camera with me. My compact does not have a very wide angle lens and I wanted to capture the scene I saw in front of me. The wide entrance narrowing down past the islands with forts and a chateau on them needed an ultra wide angle lens.

I remembered that my camera had a stitch mode and I decided to try it. It proved very easy as the camera told me what to do on the monitor screen. I was so pleased with the result that I have used it many times since.

The finished result of stitching six individual frames together. A panoramic view of the Morlaix estuary in northern France.

The six frames used to produce the Morlaix stitched picture.

Creating a spectacular wide angle photograph

The Morlaix stitch picture was the first I had attempted and I have to admit that I had ignored this option previously as a bit of a gimmick.

On my camera I select the stitch mode option from the command dial, frame my first shot and take the picture. You might have the option of choosing to shoot left to right or right to left, vertical or both – just don't do it the wrong way.

Now it gets clever and in the rear monitor it shows you the section of the last shot and the whole of what the lens is seeing. Frame the second image just so it's overlapping the first and shoot. Any misalignment will be taken care of during the merging process. If you have any form of horizon it's best to keep it level. Go on like this until you have covered the whole scene and press the finish button. Remember, the more frames you shoot the narrower and longer the picture will finish up. This could be a problem with printing out on a home printer.

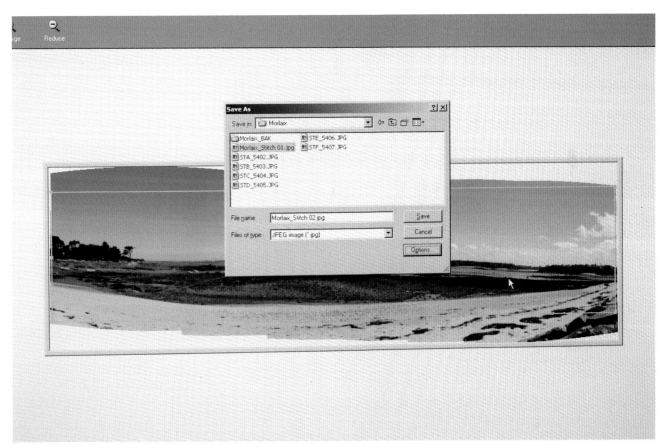

The suggested cropping of the stitched picture can be altered before being saved.

The next step is to download your images to a computer. Each set of stitched pictures will be numbered in your camera's format. Run the software program that came with your camera and choose the stitch option. This process might vary a little depending on each manufacturer's program. You select the pictures you want stitched and, as if by magic – it's great to watch on screen – the pictures are fitted together. A suggested frame for cropping is then placed around the finished area, which you can alter if so desired.

This can be repeated as many times as you want with the same pictures, so you don't lose the originals at any time. Printing out a longer length stitched picture at home could be difficult, and you might have to find a commercial lab to handle this format. They will almost certainly suggest printing to a given width with a lot of white paper top and bottom; it would be best to call and discuss the options available. If your finished result is worthy of framing then you can also obtain advice from an independent professional lab, who offer a more specialised service, on how best to do this.

Photographers on holiday can easily get bored so this is the time to experiment with some of those little used functions on the camera. Movie mode was definitely a first for me, so as I watched the seabirds flying around me, I set the movie camera into action.

The recording was in HD (high definition) and the results were astounding, quality so good that I could easily take a still from each frame and print it out at a decent size.

Keep an eye on your memory card capacity, though. The 40 second clip took up about 55Mb on my card, not an overly large amount as long as I carry large capacity cards.

Try to anticipate where a moving subject is going next to avoid losing it; this bird changed direction quickly.

Shooting movies and getting stills

There is a movie option available on your compact camera, and sometimes also available on Single Lens Reflex cameras. Some of you might be old hands with video cameras but I hadn't had much experience in this area until last year. Under a blazing sun on a hot beach, I began to experiment with my latest purchase: a Canon PowerShot G9. I was too lazy to read the instruction book, so I toyed with the controls, which were largely intuitive. I found various options for picture quality and set it to 1 ID. Everything else I set to auto.

The birds were a group of brown boobies, soaring around in circles and diving into the water. I observed them for a while and became familiar with their flight patterns; keeping my eye pressed to the viewfinder and a finger on the zoom control, I released the shutter button to start filming. Forty seconds later I had the

clearest sequence I could ever have imagined. When I played it back on a large screen it was still just as impressive. Then a thought crossed my mind – if the film was that good what would an individual frame look like?

While it is possible to stop the film and view it on the screen, I wanted to capture the frame as a JPEG (Joint Photographic Experts Group) image for printing out. A quick search on the Internet brought up several programs that could do this and some were free. I downloaded one and set it to work. It proved far simpler than I thought it would be, with many other options available.

The film is saved from your camera as an AVI (audio video interleave) file and the program, depending on which one you use, can save the selected frames into various picture formats, JPEG being the most commonly used.

Don't stop the sequence too quickly; here the bird pops up and starts to fly again. It will also give you a good margin if you need to edit the film.

The final prints were extremely good quality, not far off dedicated still shots, which surprised me.

A word here about picture formats. JPEG format is the most commonly used unless you opt to save your pictures as TIFFs or perhaps in RAW format. JPEGs work by compressing your pictures when saving them and de-compressing them when you open them. The amount of quality you lose each time depends on the degree of compression you choose.

So my advice when first downloading your pictures from your camera to a computer is to always make two sets. One should be kept as your original set – never opened, only copied to a working set which you have for everyday use. If the working set has been opened and closed many times and you need to make some prints at a later date, make a fresh set from your originals folder to obtain the very best quality.

Aspect ratio

A large ocean swell was rolling in and I took complete advantage of the conditions to produce this exciting shot of a classic yacht off Antigua. I grabbed my 300mm lens, and watching her sink down between the waves took a series of pictures as her deck disappeared from view, framing only a small section of her deck against her towering rig.

The shape of this picture or its aspect ratio is usually determined by the film or sensor size – but this is not always the case with compact cameras that can change their aspect ratio.

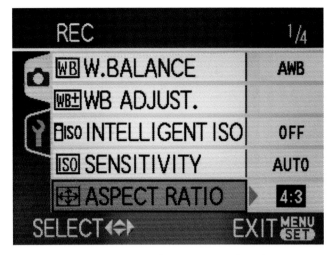

Choose your aspect ratio carefully as it has a direct bearing on the finished size and shape of your prints.

If you change your mind later, you can convert photographs already taken into another aspect ratio.

Aspect ratio – why does it matter?

The aspect ratio is the length divided by the height of your picture. In still cameras, the most common aspect ratios are 4:3 (1.33:1), 3:2 (1.5:1) and, more recently, 16:9 (1.78:1), which is also the HD format for television in Europe and most other parts of the world.

In the days of 35mm camera film the aspect ratio was 3:2 and, while you might not think this too important, it determines the full frame finished size for your colour prints. Printing papers were made in this AR as 35mm was by far the most common camera format.

Therefore you could produce a 12in ×18in print from the full frame of your negative without cropping it.

Digital compact cameras differ in that their sensors are not a full frame size; they are usually about two thirds of a conventional 35mm camera. Their AR conforms to 4:3 and the corresponding print sizes are a little more square. When you send your pictures away for printing with one of the large commercial services there is a two category price list, one for conventional sizes with an AR of 3:2 and one for digital sizes with an AR of 4:3.

I always make a point of taking my camera ashore, especially as compacts are now so small and of such good quality. You can even thread a small camera case through a belt loop to keep your hands free for important and awkward moments like balancing along a rickety pontoon. However, keep your eyes open and don't forget to capture that unusual subject or scene.

So it was that walking along a pontoon after a brisk morning sail, I spotted this beautiful scene. The gentle breeze across the water gave an almost Impressionist look to the reflection of the bright orange building. I kept the outboard engines in the shot to give it a sense of place.

If you photograph a scene that has a wide horizon, make sure you choose the correct aspect ratio to do your print justice.

Captions

I took this picture while hanging over the stern of another boat using a wide angle 28mm lens, as the other boat drove up astern passing within six foot of us. The wide angle lens distorts the image dramatically, giving that elongated-looking perspective. The drama of the picture is increased by our own powerboat's wash hitting the side of the one being photographed.

Exposure was critical; the meter reading was taken from the white hull which ensured detail in the white and darkened the background to give a dramatic effect. A fast shutter speed is necessary for fast-moving objects and to capture droplets of spray. This was shot at a shutter speed of around 1/2000 sec.

This picture was taken at the end of a two week cruise around the Grenadines in the Caribbean. When we got back to the marina at Castries on St Lucia I think I spent some time on the white yacht but it could have been the dark blue one! Framing this shot with the overhanging palm trees, which just mask the rigs, brings your eye down to the impressive charter yacht's decks. Overlaying a date is an option but only add it on a spare frame as it will detract from the final picture.

Adding the date and time to each photograph is possible but may detract visually from the final result.

Setting captions

At the end of a summer charter when the final sail has been completed, you often arrive back at the dock with the bare minimum of time to jump in a taxi and head for the plane. But try to spare a few minutes to grab the camera, go for a short walk, and take in the special surroundings that will remind you and your friends of your trip.

One option on digital cameras is the feature that can overlay the date and time, but use it sparingly as it will show up on all your prints. Perhaps it would be best shot as an extra frame so that you have the option of printing it without the caption.

There is a lot of extra information stored with your pictures, rather like an attached text file. The technical term for this is EXIF (Exchangeable Image File Format). This is now a standard amongst camera manufacturers for storing all sorts of information, including time and date. If the software you use cannot access EXIF data there are many free EXIF reader programs available on the Internet – just do a search for them on Google.

Another standard that you might see is IPTC – International Press Telecommunications Council. It was developed in the early Nineties but is seen more in the commercial world.

You may not realise that the date and time is stored as electronic information within each digital frame.

Some of the common sets of information found in an EXIF file are:

Date and time information Digital cameras will record the date and time of when you took the photograph. Remember to have the correct time and date set – for ease I use local time when I am out of the GMT zone. As an extra it will also show the time and date of the last modifications you made to your picture.

Camera settings This records the camera model, make and variable information such as orientation, aperture, shutter speed, focal length, metering mode, flash settings and ISO information. You will also find a thumbnail for previewing the picture on the camera's LCD screen plus areas for descriptions and copyright information which you can add manually. Some cameras now support GPS positioning and the lat/long of the shot can be recorded.

Multi displays

This shot of the anchored yacht does not fill the frame. This helps to convey the beauty of the surroundings. It was taken off Green Island, Antigua, and as we swung to our anchor I framed the island centrally behind the other anchored yacht. The use of a polarising filter helped darken the sky and it takes your attention towards the central subject.

The exposure reading was taken off the white hull of the yacht using the spot meter function in the camera, to avoid the picture becoming too light and over-exposed. Rather than just shooting an upright of the boat, I have allowed space around it which gives atmosphere and brings the picture to life. You just want to be there!

The multi display option is a useful way to look through the images on your memory card, and find the frame you are seeking.

Revealing multi displays

A popular feature of digital cameras is their ability to show you the shot you have just taken. I remember people keeping the same roll of film in their cameras for a whole year, but now, instead of waiting for your pictures to be processed, you can see your snaps instantly.

There is a temptation to shoot more frames than you would with a film camera, but it enables you to finely tune an exposure, or try some experimental shots.

All this, combined with the relatively low cost of camera memory cards, can lead to a veritable glut of frames that sometimes prove difficult to find later. A way round this is to use the multi display function. On my compact this is a dual control lever that, when in preview mode, uses the zoom lever with an icon like a chequered flag.

This brings up nine small images and by pressing it again brings up the previous nine, and so on. This is a useful and quick way to navigate around the hundreds of pictures stored on your memory card.

On each screen of nine, one of these images will be highlighted and by pressing the zoom lever the opposite way, towards the magnifying glass icon, you can zoom into the picture.

There is another control – a small toggle switch – that moves you around inside the image at that magnification. This is very useful if you want to check the sharpness or exposure of a small part of the picture, or red-eye in portrait shots, and gives you the opportunity to correct any mistakes.

Another glorious location but this time shot from a bike I borrowed from the marina manager. I was cycling around the island of Tahaa or Vanilla Island in French Polynesia one Sunday morning, a truly magical place, when I heard the most beautiful singing coming from this tin roofed church across the small bay. By chance a colourful dinghy was sailing by in the distance and just for a few moments this wonderful tranquil scene was the best place to be on Earth.

Categories

People are valuable subjects in sailing pictures and some like to have their photographs taken. I chose to crop in tightly on the crew, each tending to his job, on this classic yacht with her small cosy cockpit. I also used a long lens to give greater emphasis in that congested area.

As she sank down between the waves the parallel lines of green sea, varnished brown deck, blue sky and white sails appeared like an artist's canvas of coloured brush strokes. People always look better when they are sailing hard as they tend not to look at the camera. This dispenses with the resulting cheesy grin, which will ruin even the prettiest-looking yacht.

If you have shot your pictures in scene mode, one of the many additional features that digital cameras offer is the ability to sort your pictures into categories. Buried in the menu system is a category option which, when selected, will look similar to the picture on p129: a group of icons based around your particular camera's modes, the usual ones being portrait, scenery, night etc. On the Lumix camera I used for this, I highlighted the category option or I could have selected all icons. The number of pictures on your card will determine how long this operation takes.

Some of the small icons have turned a darker blue than others, indicating that pictures have been found for this category. When the search is complete you can then play back the pictures grouped in their categories or run them as a slide show. This is a useful feature when you are away from your computer as you can easily isolate a specific set of pictures, without having to hunt through all the images on your card. It's even possible to select particular images to put into a favourite group which then makes presenting them as a slide show even easier.

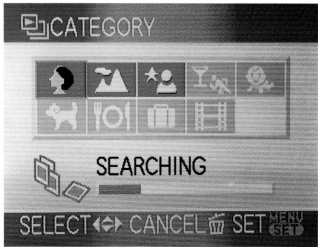

The highlighted dark blue icons show that pictures have been allocated to that category.

Pictures from other categories are easily found.

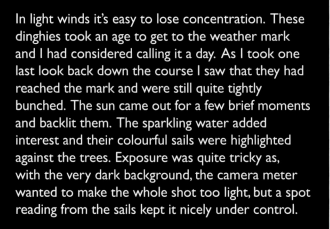

In light winds it's easy to lose concentration. These dinghies took an age to get to the weather mark and I had considered calling it a day. As I took one last look back down the course I saw that they had reached the mark and were still quite tightly bunched. The sun came out for a few brief moments and backlit them. The sparkling water added interest and their colourful sails were highlighted against the trees. Exposure was quite tricky as, with the very dark background, the camera meter wanted to make the whole shot too light, but a spot reading from the sails kept it nicely under control.

Connecting to a PC

This picture was taken on a Greek flotilla trip in the Northern Sporades. The quiet conditions early one morning allowed us to tie up together, forming a sunflower. I was hoisted up the mast of a bigger boat and this stunning image presented itself. Exposure proved tricky – as you can see, all the detail is in the white hulls and the sea is very dark.

I didn't go to the very top of the mast as I wanted to include the angles of the red forestays disappearing at the top of picture. It was shot on a 24mm wide-angle lens, and the shutter speed wasn't very fast as I was using a small aperture to keep most of the yachts and the forestays sharp.

The last day of a 'boys' winter charter and I could not sleep beyond 6am, owing to the freezing cold and having no food onboard. The tempting smells from the boulangerie along the road were compelling. In the marina the subtlest of light was breaking over the horizon, painting the whole scene, first blue then pink pastel colours as the sun got higher. A drifting dinghy was the first to get my attention, set against a mirror-like reflection. French bread tastes even better after a hard morning's work!

Downloading your pictures to a computer can be done directly from your digital camera without having to remove the memory card. However, a dedicated memory card reader is often much quicker.

Connecting to a PC

I have been using computers since 1984 and am one of the few professional photographers using a PC instead of the more widely chosen Mac. It's what I got to know in early days of computers and have kept with them ever since. It's funny how things come full circle. When I started out in 1965 black and white was the norm and colour was used sparingly but I soon realised that one day it would be the other way around and I would have to adapt or be left behind.

Who could have foreseen that in a relatively short space of time photographic film would be consigned to the bin and digital photography would rampage through barriers that existed for nearly two centuries since Niepce invented the camera obscura. Again, you either embrace the new technology or remain in the past.

When a roll of film was finished it was sent to the processing lab and back came a set of colour prints. The negatives were then carefully filed away for future prints. How many of us do that now? Digital photography has allowed us to have so many other options.

Your pictures are now stored on a memory card that has seemingly endless capacity. However, you still need to file them and keep them safe.

You have the choice of either connecting your camera to a computer – usually with a USB cable, or taking out the memory card and loading it into a card reader. You can then connect this to your computer. I have found the latter to be much quicker if I have a quantity of pictures to transfer.

The next thing to do is to make sure you can retrieve your images for future use. It is essential to understand the basic filing structure of your computer; it is not that difficult. If you are using a PC, open Windows Explorer, find your C drive and make a directory called Pictures. There is already one called My Pictures nestling down in My Documents but you will have to find it, so try this first to get the idea.

I file everything in separate directories/folders with the name of the job, location or any label that allows me to retrieve it at a later date. It is very confusing to put everything in one general file. Eventually you will have thousands of images and some of these may start to be overwritten when the numerical sequences start to repeat themselves.

Within that folder make another directory called Original Pics and copy another set to it; now you have two complete sets. One is for everyday use, viewing and an initial set of prints; the other is a pristine set, which will never be opened. This original set will be kept specially for copying a new set to a new directory to keep the JPEGs in pristine condition. This is because JPEGs lose information every time they are opened and closed (due to the amount of compression used).

To view your newly downloaded pictures, navigate back to the folder in Windows Explorer and change the View Type to Thumbnails. This option is useful for a quick check but there are much better software products available to do this. An Internet search on 'photo viewing software' will bring up hundreds, many of which are free. Some of these products have features that allow you to colour correct, crop, make slide shows and display EXIF information as well as file and edit them.

If there is a structure to your picture filing you will get so much more pleasure from viewing them, showing them to friends and, of course, getting those all-important prints from your favourite shots. Otherwise it's back to that 'it's here somewhere' routine and you will get bored and soon lose interest.

Printing tricky subjects

Not many of you would paint your house this colour but under the tropical sun it's truly vibrant. I saw this image, set on a beach to-die-for and I couldn't resist practically filling the frame with the stunning bright orange wall.

The rickety dinghy in its contrasting green was delightfully positioned, sitting tightly against the bottom of the frame with a hint of a beach and almost cloudless blue sky.

These images are easily passed by but the resulting print has given my loo wall a splash of much needed colour and a little inspiration during our grey winter.

135

It was the clearest of nights and I was on watch, doing a passage across the Bay of Biscay. The moon was shining so brightly it seemed like daytime. I keep a camera to hand for times like this and started to try some angles around the cockpit. I set the camera with a high ISO setting of 1600 so that I could get just enough speed to hand-hold it. I then exposed it to keep just enough detail in the sea and sky to show the conditions. It produced an eerie silhouetted shot reminiscent of sailing alone, enhanced by the backlit moon.

I have used this non-photo printer from Hewlett Packard and have been impressed with its speed, quality and ease of use. Reliability so far has been excellent and it is quiet in operation.

Getting the best results from your printer

If you choose to do your own photographic printing be prepared to spend quite a lot of time and money perfecting it. You can obtain good proof quality results from most printers using ordinary paper. This would be a good starting point if you have not attempted this before. To achieve near laboratory quality prints you will need to invest in a photo quality printer.

The most popular type of printer is the dot matrix and this technology uses separate ink cartridges for more precise control of colours, spraying the ink onto the paper through tiny nozzles. To really benefit you need to print onto photographic-quality paper, which comes in a variety of surface finishes, and gives excellent results at a relatively low cost.

If you have the option of a laser printer this will be the next step but, beware, running costs can be very much higher. Laser printers use a similar technology to photocopiers where toner from a cartridge is fused onto the paper. These operate much quicker than dot matrix printers. It's a personal choice but if you are buying one especially for your prints then insist on a hands-on demonstration and don't rely on the shiny sales prints shown to you by a salesman – they are practically impossible to reproduce.

I have found that some printers will work straight out of the box while others are tiresome to set up and operate – the most popular ones are not necessarily the best. To obtain good colour prints the print heads must be in perfect alignment, otherwise you get over-lapping lines of colour, or banding as it is generally known. There are various settings to correct this, depending on the type of printer, but it can be fiddly to do and when it does happen I often find it's the ink cartridge that needs replacing.

Another potential fault is ink not flowing out of the heads correctly. Usually this happens with inkjet printers which have not been used for a while so the ink dries over some of the tiny holes in the spray nozzles. Again, there is a maintenance sequence to follow which cleans them.

Now that you have your printer correctly set up, make sure you send the best possible quality image from your computer and that it matches the paper size for your print. This is where I do a few test prints on ordinary paper before committing to the expensive photographic stuff.

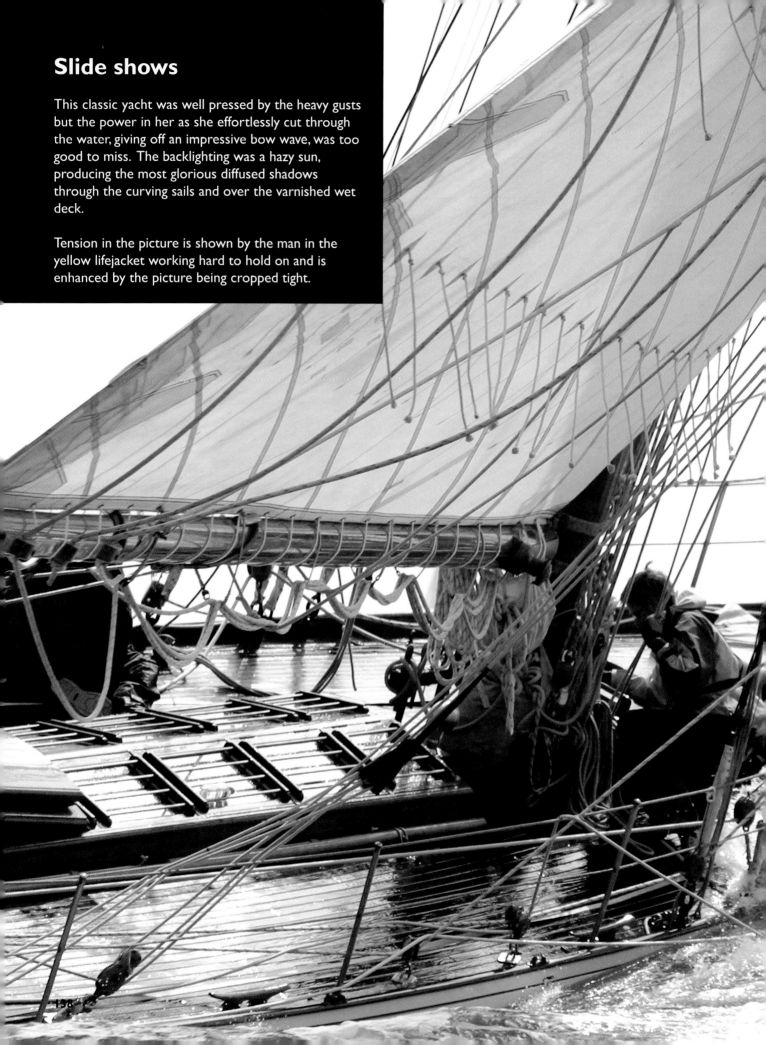

Slide shows

This classic yacht was well pressed by the heavy gusts but the power in her as she effortlessly cut through the water, giving off an impressive bow wave, was too good to miss. The backlighting was a hazy sun, producing the most glorious diffused shadows through the curving sails and over the varnished wet deck.

Tension in the picture is shown by the man in the yellow lifejacket working hard to hold on and is enhanced by the picture being cropped tight.

Don't forget to take some pictures of the person photographing you.

It's always good to have the whole crew in one shot. Try to persuade a passer-by to take a few frames on your camera.

Being this close to the start line is not to everybody's taste but the first few seconds can produce some great shapes between the hulls and sails of those yachts jostling to be first over the line. I positioned myself so that the sun reflected off the laminated sails, cropping in tight on the foredecks to emphasise the action. You get the feeling that you never want to be a bow man! This is the kind of image that makes a good start to a slide show. It gives you plenty of scope with which to overlay titles etc.

Preparing a slide show

The start of a slide show needs to capture the audience's attention; while you might not be photographing yacht races, this kind of powerful opening picture can make all the difference between them wanting to see the next shot or falling asleep. How many times have we all sat through too many dull repetitive shots of someone's holiday snaps? Let's try to make it more interesting.

Firstly, choose your pictures with care. You have just finished a weekend cruise with some friends and there will be a wide variety of subjects from sailing shots, harbours visited and shore scenes etc. Now try to make up a sequence that is interesting to everyone,

balancing the people pictures with the scenes and trying to give it a sense of place.

You can make a slide show using just the camera but it's much simpler to do this on a computer. Many of the file viewing programs have a slide show option which will also allow you to add titles and music. Download your pictures and make your selection to a new folder; don't forget to give it a meaningful name. This means that you can view the whole set of pictures you will be using as they will appear on the screen. It will make future

additions or deletions easier without affecting your original image set.

If your pictures are shot at maximum resolution the images will be on the large size, so use the editing feature of your file viewing program to reduce them in size. Image size is important here. If they are too big, say over 0.5Mb, they will take a longer time to load and run, depending on the computer equipment used. Conversely, if they are too small, quality will suffer. Make sure you use a working set only and not your original set, otherwise they will be this size for ever!

The slide show program will allow you to rearrange the order in which they are shown. The next step is to decide how long each picture should last on the screen. You might also like to use the option to select the kind of dissolve/transition pattern between each picture.

With a little imagination, I think it is possible to make a very interesting slide show. You can now save the individual file, to be played again and again, put it on a DVD and send it to friends and crew as a memento of that great weekend sail.

Creating a cruising photographic log

If you plan to create a log of your cruise, take plenty of photographs of everywhere you go, and take time to capture as many scenes as you can. The objective is to be able to write an account of your visit in detail. This is one of a series of pictures taken at Pontreiux in France. The pretty group of houses was surrounded by a varied collection of different boats.

I also wanted to capture the atmosphere of all of this in one photograph, so I took the time to row the dinghy across the river, and shoot from the opposite bank.

The pleasing backdrop of the houses gave me the inspiration to crop in tight.

If you are planning a holiday, which could be a cruise in your own or a friend's boat, you have an opportunity to plan how you will record the experience. An excellent way to use the photographs you take is to create a log. This can be a very detailed account in words and pictures or a more visual record concentrating on photographs with short captions.

The example here shows what can be done using the services of one of the digital photographic companies who advertise on the Internet. You create the pages from their templates and the end result is a high quality hardback book.

Virgin Atlantic
in
Simoon III of London
15th December 2007
to
12th January 2008

A high-quality hardback record of a cruise.

The feel that can be achieved by using a wide angle lens tells a totally different story.

The pages can accommodate pictures and text to your own design (cruising log courtesy Simon Fraser).

The key to success is to decide in advance what type of log you wish to make. The most interesting for the reader is a mixture of description, anecdote and photographs. A navigational log with details of wind speed, weather, course direction etc is not the basis of an interesting record of your holiday cruise. Make lots of notes as you take the photographs and record what people say at the time.

Sepia photography

Racing boat photographs at the turn of the Twentieth Century were produced in sepia: a technique in those days involving a black and white print put through a series of chemical baths toning the black image on the print into tones of sepia.

Today this option is still available in various forms. Most digital cameras offer the option of shooting in sepia.

This picture is an example of another way of producing a sepia toned image but this time by manipulating a colour shot on the computer. Most image editing software has options for photographic effects, sepia being a popular one.

Sepia toning of photographs evolved in the Nineteenth Century, probably because early black and white film could not record solid black. The resulting black and white prints always looked soft and muddy with tones of grey lacking in contrast. Most subjects were portraits chiefly because film and shutter speed were very slow, coupled with poor image sharpness. Photographers eager to please their customers developed many different colour tints to apply to their black and white prints. The sepia colour emerged as a firm favourite due to the resemblance to skin-like colours.

When film speeds and shutters became faster, cameras were moved out of doors to photograph moving subjects. In today's digital world sepia pictures are still popular and far easier to achieve. The results shot on camera produce a pleasing effect but lack any form of control. Varying the sepia effect is best achieved on your photo editing software, which gives you infinite control over contrast and sepia depth.

There are no hard and fast rules as to what is right and wrong; experiment is the order of the day as the results are purely personal taste.

I always find it interesting to look at a set of pictures and try some of them out in different colour tones. The different effects on the same picture are quite remarkable.

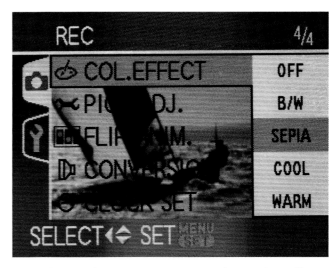

Under the recording section in your menu choose colour effect and set the sepia option.

The famous boatbuilder Alastair Garland shows off his exquisite river launch at Henley, built to the quality standards of a Stradivarius violin. This subject is very appropriate for the sepia treatment, especially as the people took the trouble to dress in period costume. I seized the opportunity to grab a few frames which I knew instantly I would be turning into a sepia print for him.

While I was photographing a friend's yacht I was trying to work out ways to make it special for him. I initially shied away from doing a whole boat portrait, and noticed that on a stiff beat he was in fairly close competition with another yacht. So I positioned myself to leeward with the sun raking across the deck, with the other yacht also in the picture.

Sometimes I set myself a deliberate challenge and with the rare opportunity to sail on the famous classic yacht *Altair*, I decided to record some of the day in black and white. It made me think in a totally different way as I then had to record tones of black rather than colour. This gave the finished portfolio of the day's sailing an unusual authentic feel.

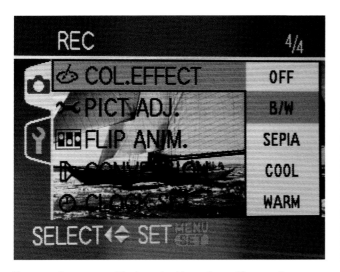

You can choose your black and white colour effect on the camera, but you might prefer to apply the change at a later stage on the computer, which gives you greater control.

Black and white photographs lend themselves to atmospheric subjects; here the photographer's eye is the most important tool.

I have a particular fondness for black and white photography. I was introduced to this medium when colour was still in its infancy. The sheer pleasure obtained from loading film in a darkroom, processing it, and then printing the negatives by hand in various hazardous chemical baths still fills me with great nostalgia.

A black and white photograph can be more creative than a colour picture and is often able to convey atmosphere to the subject not apparent in an ordinary colour image. Colour contains so much information that it sometimes confuses the story you wish to tell; black and white allows you to change the shot's emphasis by increasing the contrasts of shape and form.

Today black and white is gaining popularity, with many exhibitions being shown in this medium. It can suit all sorts of subjects from lonely landscapes to detailed portraits. It can give a special feeling and a touch of class to quite ordinary images. Only the dedicated and usually professional photographer shoots with black and white film, partly because of the difficulty in getting it processed. A digital camera can handle this medium very easily without buying expensive processing materials.

Alternatively, if you decide at a later date that you would like to make a black and white image of your favourite sailing shot, it is a relatively simple process on a computer with an image-editing program. There are many programs available, starting with free ones from Internet download sites right through to the top of the range professional ones like Adobe Photoshop. Practically all these programs have options to turn your colour pictures into black and white. They offer far greater control than the conversion process made in a camera, allowing you more freedom for creativity.

A useful tip I have found, when converting pictures on a computer to black and white, is not to convert them to a grey scale image but to desaturate the colour image so that it appears black and white. This process is usually carried out through the hue/saturation option by reducing saturation to zero. I can then add colour back into the picture in any amount I choose. This allows me to have complete control over the tonal range and depth of colour to suit my requirements.

Summary of tips

Tips for taking better photographs

- Compact cameras have built-in flash and are best with zoom lenses.
- APS is not as popular as manufacturers had hoped.
- SLR's main advantage – interchangeable lenses.
- Zoom lenses are equal in quality to fixed focal length lenses.
- Buy lenses with the smallest f number you can afford.
- Zoom lenses have great versatility but are bulkier.
- Always use a skylight filter for lens protection on SLRs.
- Exercise discretion when using polarising and graduated filters.
- Keep your camera bag small – otherwise you will not be inclined to carry it around.
- Check your lens/filter and clean regularly.
- Always carry a spare battery.
- Splashproof – best suited type, ideally with a zoom lens.

Sometimes pictures present themselves to you unexpectedly but you might need to be quick. I have always advocated having a camera as part of a yacht's inventory for those unforeseen moments.

Having just tied up in the old harbour and sitting in the cockpit I noticed this Dutch Botter sailing past but on the other side of the high harbour wall. Keeping a small part of the grass bank, steps and a bollard in the lower part of the frame, all I could see was the top part of the white sails against the clear blue sky. It's tempting to say, 'I'll shoot that in a minute', but that minute will never present itself again.

- Read the instruction book and understand all the features.
- Flash on cameras tends to produce the red-eye effect.
- Fill-in flash produces more natural results.
- Bounce flash produces soft shadows.
- Have sufficient capacity in batteries and memory cards for your shots.
- Keep fingers off the lens and flash when taking shots.
- Press shutter gently to avoid camera shake.
- Move around your boat with safety in mind.
- Don't take your eye away until after the shutter has closed.
- Check your focus point is positioned over your subject.
- Don't issue continuous instructions – it ruins naturalness.
- Take in surroundings to place your shot.
- Auto metering gives very reliable results.
- Be prepared to adjust the exposure in difficult lighting conditions.
- Experiment with different metering modes if available on your camera.
- A hand-held meter will help you decide on the correction needed.
- What you see in the viewfinder is what you get.
- Try to use the white balance icons instead of auto WB.
- Metering systems can be confused in extreme lighting conditions.
- Try to introduce ambient light into flash pictures.
- Make sure that your focussing marks are over your subject.

- Don't buy a flash that is too big.
- Buy high capacity rechargeable batteries.
- Try using a manual meter in difficult lighting conditions.
- Keep to as small a model as possible.
- Keep a clamp onboard.
- Store the camera dry and in a well-padded bag.
- Service it occasionally, especially if well-used·

- Try to keep the sun behind or to the side of you for best results.
- Use a lens hood – check for cut-off.
- Use fill-in flash for those harsh shadows.
- Look for something different – it's all around you.
- Not only sunny days produce good colour conditions.
- Be prepared before setting off.
- Look for the unusual.
- Use the elements to your advantage.
- Look around and include the scenery, especially if you are not returning.
- Better to have 10 good ones than 100 mediocre ones.
- Try polarising or graduated filters.
- Get off your boat at interesting anchorages and take your camera.

Other important considerations

- It is not necessary to spend large sums of money on thousands of extras but camera magazines and Internet companies have lots of suggestions to help you part with your cash.
- I touched on the subject of cleaning materials earlier.

I use a clean micro-fibre cloth on the optics; this is usually sufficient if used regularly. If you need to remove dirt and heavier grease marks, a lens cleaning solution is the answer. I like to use a clean cotton towel or chamois leather for the general cleaning of camera bodies. If you get sea spray over your kit, wipe it off as soon as possible to help avoid technical failures later.

- I find a small Swiss Army knife handy for those irritating jobs like opening small battery compartments, tightening up screws etc. Failing that, a twenty pence piece can be useful.
- A small torch is useful for changing batteries or seeing the controls in dark conditions. It might even help you get back down that dimly-lit path from the pub – after you have taken that perfect picture of a sunset, of course.
- Make sure you carry two sets of batteries for everything. This way you should not get caught out. When you use the first set buy another at the next available opportunity. Keep them dry, in a small container and separated, in case they short out against each other. One of those small plastic containers with a snap-on lid is good.

Introduction.
Shot: Lyme Bay/UK – Canon EOS camera and 70–200mm f2.8 IS lens. Page 8.

Setting the camera menu.
Shot: Cumberland Bay/St Vincent/WI – Canon EOS camera and 70–200mm f2.8 IS lens. Page 14.

The LCD monitor and viewfinder.
Shot: St Quay-Portrieux/Brittany – Canon EOS camera and 17–35mm f2.8 lens. Page 18.

Taking pictures in automatic mode.
Shot: St Peter Port/Guernsey – Canon EOS camera and 70–200mm f2.8 IS lens. Page 22.

Plan your photography.
Shot: Loch Fyne/UK – Canon EOS camera and 70–200mm f2.8 IS lens. Page 26.

Taking close-ups.
Shot onboard *Kate* a replica Milne, 12M off of St Kitts/WI. 24mm lens. Page 30.

Zoom photography.
Shot: Lyme Bay/UK – Canon EOS camera and 70–200mm f2.8 IS lens. Page 34.

Night photography.
Shot: Dartmouth/UK – Canon EOS camera and 17–35mm f2.8 lens. Time exposure 8–20 seconds at f11. Page 38.

Low level light photography.
Shot: Lymington/UK – Canon EOS camera and 24–105mm lens. Page 42.

Photographing landscapes.
Shot: Prideaux Haven/Canada – Canon EOS and 24–70 f2.8 lens. Page 46.

Composing great photographs.
Shot: Nevis/WI – Canon EOS camera and 24–105 f2.8 IS lens. Page 50.

Capturing the action in auto focus.
Shot: Antigua/WI – Canon EOS camera and 300mm f4 lens. Page 54.

The importance of light, colour and exposure.
Shot: Lyme Bay/UK – Canon EOS camera and 70–200 f2.8 IS lens. Page 58.

When and how to use flash.
Shot: N coast of Grenada/WI – Canon EOS camera and 17–35mm f2.8 lens. Page 62.

Custom settings.
Shot: N coast of St Martin/WI – Canon EOS camera and 70–200 f2.8 IS lens. Page 66.

Manual exposure.
Shot: Loch Fyne/Scotland/UK – Canon EOS camera and 300mm f4 lens. Page 70.

Manual focus.
Shot: Cowes/Isle of Wight/UK – Canon EOS camera and 70–200mm f2.8 IS lens. Page 74.

Using filters.
Shot: W of Dartmouth/UK – Canon EOS camera and 70–200mm f2.8 IS lens. Page 78.

Supplementary lenses.
Shot: leaving Falmouth Bay/Antigua/WI – Canon EOS camera and 17–35mm f4 lens. Page 82.

White balance.
Shot: Skopolos/Greece – Canon EOS camera 17–35mm f2.8 lens. Page 86.

Histograms.
Shot: Loch Fyne/UK – Canon EOS camera 70–200mm f2.8 IS lens. Page 90.

ISO and why it matters.
Shot: The Med off Mallorca – Canon EOS camera and 70–200mm f2.8 IS lens. Page 94.

Boat to boat photography.
Shot: W of Dartmouth – Canon EOS camera and 70–200mm f2.8 IS lens. Page 98.

Stabilising your camera.
Shot: off entrance to Treguier/N France – Canon EOS camera and 70–200mm f2.8 IS lens. Page 102.

Panning shots joined together.
Shot: Morlaix/N France – Canon
PowerShot G9 camera. Page 106.

Movies and stills.
Shot: Anguilla/WI – Canon PowerShot G9
camera. Page 110.

Aspect ratio.
Shot: Antigua/WI – Canon EOS camera
and 70–200mm f2.8 IS lens. Page 114.

Captions.
Shot: The Solent/UK – Canon EOS camera
17–35mm f2.8 lens. Page 118.

Multi display.
Shot: Green Island/Antigua/WI – Canon
EOS camera and 70–200mm f2.8 IS lens.
Page 122.

Categories.
Shot: off Dartmouth/UK – Canon EOS
camera and 300mm f4 IS lens. Page 126.

Connecting to a PC.
Shot: N. Sporades/Greece – Canon
EOS camera and 17–35mm f2.8 IS lens.
Page 130.

Printing tricky subjects.
Shot: Boa Vista/Cape Verde Islands –
Canon PowerShot G5 camera. Page 134.

Slide shows.
Shot: off Dartmouth/UK – Canon
EOS camera and 70–200mm f2.8 IS lens.
Page 138.

Creating a cruising photographic log.
Shot: Pontrieux/France – Canon
PowerShot G5. Page 142.

Sepia photography.
Shot: The Solent/UK – Canon EOS camera
and 24–105mm f4 IS lens. Page 146.

Black and white photography.
Shot: The Solent/UK – Canon EOS camera
and 17–35mm f2.8 lens. Page 150.

Acknowledgements

I'll try not to make this page sound like the Oscars but I have received a lot of help in compiling this book. So my thanks go to:

Janet Murphy – my long suffering publisher who has stuck with me on this project, offering all sorts of advice and enthusiasm, even when my own lapses in progression threatened to de-rail the whole thing.

Fred Barter – my pictures editor: Fred's clear vision from day one and his unwavering 'Art Directors' mind helped to produce the stunning visual layout. His critical eye also helped to choose what he calls 'the most stunning collection of pictures in one book' (I could not possibly comment on this) but his dedication gave me a tremendous insight into how others see my pictures.

Joanna Pope – my partner: While I think my first attempts to write this book in English were successful, she definitely had other ideas. Together we spent many hours/days agonising over my text so that 'wot I rote' made sense to you all. I am eternally grateful to Joanna for pointing out this parallel language after all these years!

Esmée Roach – my daughter: A teenager who volunteered to spend hours helping sort out my pictures for the relevant pages, with a fastidious attention to detail not yet seen in her Father. If you need a job later Darling!

Terence Donovan – photographic mentor: For instilling in me the importance that being good is only average. The last 5% needed to be great is so very hard to achieve, whatever you do in life. Sadly he is no longer with us but his compelling magic of making each shoot a totally new challenge has remained with me.

The Sea: In the fifty odd years I have sailed and worked in this environment it has been kind to me so far.

I've sailed those wide oceans,
Five decades or more.
Now sometimes, I wonder, what I did it for
No man has the answer –
Is it pleasure or gain?
With my life in my pictures
I'd do it again!

Roach Sea Shanty – J Pope 2009